AN EVENING WITH GARY LINEKER

and

TRENCH KISS

AN EVENING WITH GARY LINEKER

by Arthur Smith
and
Chris England

and

TRENCH KISS

by Arthur Smith

JOSEF WEINBERGER PLAYS

LONDON

ARTHUR SMITH

Arthur Smith was born in 1954 in Bermondsey, London. After university he did low-paid jobs by day, and sang in a band and appeared in Fringe revues by night. In the 1980s he turned to stand-up comedy in a double act with Phil Nice and as a solo comedian and compère. His first play was *Live Bed Show* (1989), first staged at the Edinburgh Festival Fringe and subsequently in London at the Donmar Warehouse, Lyric Theatre, Hammersmith and in the West End at the Garrick Theatre, starring Paul Merton and Caroline Quentin. His other plays include *Sod*, and, with Tony Hawks, the lecture/play *Arthur Smith sings Andy Williams*.

CHRIS ENGLAND

Chris England studied English Literature at Pembroke College, Cambridge, where he joined Cambridge Footlights and toured the UK and Australia with the revue *Hawaiian Cheese Party*. He then co-founded Bad Lib Theatre Company, co-writing a number of new plays including *Feeling the Benefit, The Preventers* and *Return of the Preventers*. He has also written for TV, co-writing the series *Revolting Animals, Jellyneck* and *All Change! An Evening with Gary Lineker* is his first collaboration with Arthur Smith. Chris supports Oldham Athletic.

An Evening With Gary Lineker first published in 1992 by
Josef Weinberger Ltd (pka Warner/Chappell Plays Ltd)
12-14 Mortimer Street, London, W1T 3JJ

Trench Kiss first published in 1992 by
Josef Weinberger Ltd (pka Warner/Chappell Plays Ltd)
12-14 Mortimer Street, London, W1T 3JJ

ISBN 0 85676 129 X

Reprinted 1993, 2001

Printed by Commercial Colour Press Plc, London E7

AN EVENING WITH GARY LINEKER

Arthur Smith
and
Chris England

An Evening With Gary Lineker was first performed at the Bath
Festival on June 7th, 1991. The production, by Incidental Theatre,
then appeared at the Assembly Rooms in Edinburgh as part of the
1991 Edinburgh Fringe Festival, and at the Purcell Rooms in London
as part of the Pick of the Fringe season in October, 1991. The
original cast was as follows:

Monica	Caroline Quentin
Bill	Andy Taylor
Ian	Chris England
Birgitta	Maria McErlane
Dan	Nick Hancock

Directed by   Audrey Cooke

An Evening With Gary Lineker subsequently opened in the West
End at the Duchess Theatre on 19th December, 1991, co-produced by
Incidental Theatre and PW Productions. In the West End the part of
Monica was played initially by Morwenna Banks, and then later by
Caroline Quentin as before. The part of Gary Lineker was played in
Bath by Arthur Smith, in Edinburgh by Tony Hawks, and in London
by Niall Ashdown. Otherwise the cast and director remained the
same, and the production was designed by Andrew Leigh. The play
was nominated Comedy of the Year in the 1992 Olivier Awards.

AUTHOR'S NOTE:

"An Evening With Gary Lineker" has, appropriately enough, two
forty-five minute halves - give or take a little injury time here and
there. The show started life, however, as a one act play around
seventy-five minutes long, and if you want to perform that shorter
piece you could simply remove the chunk that we added without
significantly harming the story. To do this, cut from:

On page 22 where Bill says "Sixteen minutes . . . "

        to

On page 31 where Bill says "Yeah, yeah . . . "

You will also need to lose Birgitta's references to Roger Milla,
"King of the Road" on page 34 and to her crush on Kevin Keegan on
page 44.

Part One

The lights rise to reveal MONICA *standing and facing the audience.*
BILL *is sitting behind her, not looking at her, watching TV in a*
tableau of 'relationship-not-working'. Both are around thirty years
old. A somewhat tense silence for a few moments, then MONICA
decides to speak.

MONICA   Bill? I'm leaving you. I'm sorry it's come to this, I
              never meant to hurt you, but I'm certain it's best for
              both of us.

BILL   (*at the television set*) Ooooh! You bastard!

MONICA   I'll pack some things together and go tonight. I can
              come back for the rest of my stuff some time when
              you're out.

BILL   Sorry, love, can this wait till half time? I can't really
              concentrate on what you're saying.

              (MONICA *goes and switches the television off.*)

MONICA   Bill? I'm leaving you. I'm sorry it's come to this, I
              never meant to hurt you. But I'm certain it's best for
              both of us.

BILL   Oh. What will you do about your things?

MONICA   I'll pack some things together and go tonight. I can
              come back for the rest of my stuff some time when
              you're out.

BILL   Will you go to Pam's? Or is there . . . someone else?

MONICA   There's someone else.

BILL   Do I know him?

MONICA   Sort of.

BILL   Sort of? I sort of know him?

MONICA   Yes, sort of.

BILL   A mate of mine, is it? Ian? Not Ian?

MONICA   No.

BILL   Do I like him, this bloke?

MONICA   Yes you like him.

BILL   (*attempting to make her smile*) Definitely not Ian,
then.

MONICA   Bill. I'm leaving you, after eight years of sometimes
not too unhappy marriage, and I'm going to live with
Gary Lineker.

BILL   Oh. I'd never have got that.

MONICA   Do you understand me? I'm going to live with Gary
Lineker.

BILL   Of Spurs and England, yes.

(*Pause.*)

MONICA   Aren't you going to say anything?

BILL   I'm stunned. Congratulations!

MONICA   What?

BILL   Gary Lineker, eh? Well done! That's brilliant!

MONICA   You're upset, I can see that . . .

BILL   No I'm not! I mean, anybody else, obviously, it would
have been a blow, but . . . Gary Lineker! I mean,
look at his record. Thirty one goals in fifty one
internationals, the guy's a hero. I hope you'll be very
happy together.

MONICA   Thank you. (*Pause.*) I'll go and collect some things
together. Will you be all right?

BILL   Me? I'll be fine, don't worry about me.

MONICA   Are you sure?

BILL   Oh yes. There's the second half in a minute, and
then there's all the goals from yesterday.

(MONICA *comes forward and talks straight out to the audience.* BILL *switches TV back on and sits in front of it.*)

MONICA   See? If it was as easy as that I'd do it tomorrow. If I was having an affair with Gary Lineker it would be just really easy to know what I wanted to do. But I'm not. So it isn't.

BILL   Monica?

MONICA   Yes?

BILL   Are you going to get married to him, do you think?

MONICA   I don't know.

BILL   'Cos if you did, you'd be Monica Lineker. Ha ha ha ha. (*He goes back to watching the television.*)

MONICA   (*to audience*) It's not that I'm certain that I want things to go on the way they are. It's just that I'm not certain that if I change things, they'll be any better.

(*The lights change to reveal that they are in a hotel room. The previous scene, in* MONICA'S *imagination, has taken place at their home. The hotel room is the living room of a small but quite expensive suite. It has two seats and a sofa arranged around the television. A door leads off to the bedroom and the balcony, and another leads to a sort of small kitchenette. A third doorway leads out to a little corridor, which is the way out to the rest of the hotel, and the toilet/ bathroom is out this way too. There is a telephone, and* BILL *has stuck a home-made World Cup wall chart on the wall.*)

It is July 4th, 1990, we are in a hotel in Majorca. It is England versus West Germany in the semi-final of the World Cup, and this . . .

(*She indicates* BILL *who is now writing something on a piece of paper on the wall.*)

. . . is my husband Bill. He is a mature man, a man respected in the world of publishing. He has a first class degree in English literature from York University, and at the moment he is filling in his World Cup wall chart. This is his second World Cup wall chart. His original World Cup wall chart caught fire in mysterious circumstances. Annoyingly, he was actually pleased to have to do it all over again.

I do talk to Bill. And Bill talks to me. But we're so busy talking to each other that we never talk to each other.

(MONICA *goes into the room and sits down. She picks up a magazine, sniffs her blouse.*)

I can still smell pickled onions.

BILL   What a great day you're having.

MONICA   (*tuts*) I've washed this four times. Do you know every time we've been out in the last two weeks I've had to use two bottles of perfume.

BILL   I'd kill for a fag now.

MONICA   Nina Ricci nil, Sarsons' famous pickling vinegar six.

(BILL *breaks off from amending his wall chart and looks at his watch.*)

BILL   Thirty nine minutes to kick off. I'd best get the beers in.

(*During the next few minutes* BILL *continues talking, while bringing on an improbable amount of beer and snacks.*)

MONICA   They weren't even our pickled onions. We were smuggling them.

BILL   Oh come on, Monica, don't start with the pickled onions again. It was an accident. No one wanted the top to come off in your suitcase.

MONICA   What breed of man is it who takes pickled onions on holiday with him?

BILL   He didn't have room in his bag.

MONICA   That's his trouble, Ian . . . He's never got room in his
              bag.

BILL   I hope you realise that doesn't actually mean
              anything at all. Look, I'm sorry about the Ian
              business, but you invited him too.

MONICA   Yes, but I didn't invite his pickled onions.

BILL   Listen, Ian is . . . I don't want to make another speech
              about Ian.

MONICA   Good, because I don't want to hear another one.

BILL   He was my . . . (MONICA *joins in.*) . . . best friend at
              school. (BILL *pauses.*) He's got a good heart.

              (MONICA *looks at him, laughs bitterly.*)

              Can I have a cigarette if England score?

MONICA   No, certainly not.

BILL   Come on, this is the most exciting night of the year. I
              didn't have one during the Cameroons. I bet Bobby
              Charlton did.

MONICA   Bobby Charlton?

BILL   A bloke told me once that Bobby Charlton is a sixty
              a day man. He used to have one at half time. So I
              could have just one.

MONICA   You're not Bobby Charlton.

BILL   No, and neither is Bobby Charlton if he hasn't had a
              fag. Couldn't I have one if the Germans score? Have
              we got that many? No, just the one . . .

MONICA   Oh, have one. Have the packet, I don't care. I'm
              going to.

              (*She lights one from the packet she has thrown him.
              He didn't expect this. Puts one in his mouth
              tentatively, but doesn't light it.*)

BILL   I don't want it now.

MONICA   I bet Gary Lineker doesn't smoke.

BILL   He doesn't fart he's so perfect. And if he does they smell of perfume. Gary Lineker - the Queen Mother of football.

MONICA   He a got nice legs and a nice smile, and most men get away with a lot less than that.

BILL   Do you think I've got a nice smile? (*Does his nice smile, which* MONICA *doesn't really react to.*) I bet Gary Lineker doesn't snore.

MONICA   I can't help it, you know I can't.

BILL   I know. One of the first things you ever said to me was "I snore like a wildebeest with a drink problem".

MONICA   Yes, I used to say that.

BILL   It was a real turn on, actually.

(MONICA *looks away.*)

Thirty seven minutes. The teams will be in the changing rooms now. Michael's there in Italy, you know.

MONICA   I know.

BILL   I hope he hasn't got in, the bastard.

MONICA   It's still not too late to go for a quiet meal somewhere.

BILL   You're joking aren't you? Every restaurant on the island will have this on the telly, it's the World Cup semi-final. That cab I got back last night, the driver had the match on a little telly on the dashboard and we were watching it as we were going along. Ridiculous. So tiny you couldn't really see the ball or anything.

MONICA   Who was driving?

BILL   Oh he was doing most of the footwork. We took it in turns to steer.

MONICA   Sounds really dangerous. Do you think Ian will come by cab?

(BILL *snorts*.)

BILL   I'm getting quite nervous now. In two hours we could be in the World Cup final.

MONICA   The Germans are going to win.

(BILL *is a little alarmed*.)

BILL   Do you know?

MONICA   No.

BILL   We've got a chance. I mean, you'd never have thought Argentina could get through.

MONICA   Yes, poor old Italy. They were so lovely those Italians. What's the name of the one I fancied?

BILL   Giannini.

MONICA   Giannini. Why can't you be Italian?

BILL   You're so fickle. Five minutes ago it was Gary Lineker, now you're off with some long-haired lothario.

MONICA   Well, Gary's going to be away a lot. I'll need a lover.

BILL   Won't Gazza do?

MONICA   Gazza? Please!

BILL   Do you think the seating is right? I'll sit here, I think. Hang on, I'll try it.

(*He sits down. Then leaps up as though England have scored.*)

Goooooaalllll!!! Incredible! Peter Shilton has scored for England! Yup, that's the one.

MONICA   I'll sit here. I might be in and out.

BILL   It's the World Cup semi-final, you know.

MONICA	Yes. Football, isn't it?
BILL	That's good, actually, because it puts Ian next to the lovely Birgitta.
MONICA	Ugh! Why do you always have to call her "the lovely Birgitta"?
BILL	Well . . . she is lovely, isn't she?
MONICA	That's how *he* talks, "the lovely Birgitta". You sound just like him sometimes.
BILL	Well I haven't referred to her as my "Teutonic sidekick" yet.
MONICA	God, I couldn't believe it when he said that.
BILL	It *was* gross . . .
MONICA	Careful! Nearly criticised him then, that would never do.
BILL	Ian is an irritating man, I know that.
MONICA	So why do you have him around all the time?
BILL	Well where else is he going to go?
MONICA	What do I care?
BILL	Well, enough to spend most of your holiday talking about him. I think Birgitta does fancy him, you know.
MONICA	Is that why she spent two hours on the dance floor with you last night?
BILL	We were talking about him.
MONICA	Better than talking *to* him, which is what you left me doing.
	(*Pause.*)
BILL	So you think she doesn't fancy him, then?
MONICA	Well, I mean look at her. She spends her whole time in that sexy red outfit surrounded by gorgeous

tanned German men, all of whom would ritually
sacrifice their mothers just to touch her . . .

BILL   Yeah, and then brag about it to all the others, very
              appealing. Besides she's the rep and they're the
              clients. Their status is too low.

MONICA   What sort of status has Ian got? He's an ugly, boring,
              humourless, sad, poor little failure.

BILL   Now come on, he's not little. And ours not to reason
              why. Maybe they share a love of pickled vegetables,
              she is German after all . . .

MONICA   Yes, and it's England versus West Germany. Why
              would she want to watch it with a bunch of English
              people. If Germany win you'll probably sling her off
              the balcony.

BILL   Oh yeah.

MONICA   You know how you get during football games.

BILL   I'm not going to hit her though, am I? (MONICA *says
              nothing*.) Unless they win on penalties, of course,
              then I'll cut her throat the goose-stepping bitch.

MONICA   Are we going to talk, do you think?

BILL   I expect so. Unless it's a really dull game. I expect
              something will come up, some topic of interest . . .

MONICA   I don't mean about the game. We've been here for
              two weeks and I thought the whole point was that
              we'd have the opportunity to spend some time . . .
              Bill? Bill?

              (BILL *has gone vacant. He is miles away. He has lost
              the plot. Then there is a knock at the door*.)

BILL   Ah, the crowd are arriving! Thirty one minutes to go.
              (*Goes to door, chanting in vaguely Italian accent*.)
              Sheelton! Sheelton! Go and get your keelt on,
              Sheelton!

              (*He opens the door.* IAN *enters carrying a plastic
              bag. He is around thirty, dressed sensibly and*

unimaginatively, perhaps in one of those short-sleeved shirts people wear in the summer in the office. He is not tanned, and is rather sweaty.)

Ian. Give me an S!

IAN   I don't like football, you know that.

BILL   Is Birgitta not with you?

IAN   Ah, the lovely Birgitta. (MONICA *rolls her eyes heavenwards.*) My Teutonic sidekick. (MONICA *groans audibly.*) She's not, no.

MONICA   We can see that. Where is she?

IAN   She knows where it is. She'll get a cab or something when she's good and ready. You know what women are like. Obviously. You are one. I brought some beer.

           (IAN *takes one bottle of beer out of the bag and puts it on the table. Screws the bag up.*)

BILL   Thanks.

IAN   And I brought you a present, Monica.

MONICA   Oh.

IAN   Here. (*Gives her some perfume.*) It's some perfume.

MONICA   Oh. Thank you.

IAN   Someone left it behind in my new hotel room. Birgitta didn't want it so I thought I might as well give it to you. You still smell quite a lot of pickled onions, I don't know whether you noticed that. I was quite surprised they found me a new room really quickly.

BILL   I should hope so. It's not as if it was your fault the roof fell in. What's it like?

IAN   Oh it's not bad, really, once you get used to it. You go in, close the door, and then if you push the bed up against the door - well, you sort of have to pull it half the way, then get over it, then push it - then you can open the drawers of the wardrobe nearly all the way out, and you've got your own little bathroom which you get to either by climbing over the table or crawling under the table. And the bathroom's rather ingenious, actually, because it's only like this big (*Indicates a four foot square cubicle.*) The sink's here, right, and the toilet's right underneath, and the pipe from the plughole goes straight into the toilet, which makes it rather difficult to sit on the toilet when you want to . . . you know . . . sit on the toilet.

BILL   What, for a shit or something like that?

IAN   Yes, and the shower's just in the wall right here by the sink, with taps here, and also down by the floor, which I didn't get at first, but when I tried them they turned the toilet into a bidet. Ingenious. I couldn't work it out to start with, and on the first night when I cleaned my teeth all the spit went down the plughole, out of the pipe, and into my slippers, but I think I've got the hang of it now. In fact you'll never guess what I did this morning. I, simultaneously, had a sh . . . a . . . sh . . . it, a shower, a shampoo, and a shave.

BILL   Fantastic.

IAN   I thought so. I couldn't think of anything else that begins with shhh that I could do, or I'd have done it.

MONICA   You could have shot yourself . . .

(BILL *and* MONICA *exchange a glance.* MONICA *tuts and leaves the room onto the balcony.*)

BILL   Well at least it's better than the building site you were in.

(*Lights up on* MONICA *on the balcony. She addresses the audience.*)

MONICA   The thing about Gary is . . . nothing ever gets him down. He's so level and even-tempered. It's not just a physical thing with me and Gary. I can really talk to him. I know what you're thinking. You're thinking: "What sort of a conversation can she have with Gary Lineker?" Well, we can talk about more or less anything. I tell him about Bill, and how I just can't bear the thought of going on the way things are, and he says: "It's all about ninety minutes on the day, Monica. The game's never over until the final whistle's blown." And you know he's right.

(*Lights up on* BILL *and* IAN *back in the room.*)

BILL   So what does Birgitta think of it?

IAN   You what?

BILL   Birgitta . . . what does she think of your room?

IAN   Oh I see. I thought you meant what does she think of . . . you know . . . *it* . . .

BILL   Well you can tell me that in a minute. What does she think of your room?

IAN   Well I don't know.

BILL   You don't mean to tell me you haven't taken her back to your room?

IAN   Why would I want to do that? There's hardly room to swing a cat in there.

BILL   Has she got a cat?

IAN   No.

BILL   Well so what? If there's a bed there's room to make the two-backed beast.

IAN   The what?

BILL   The two-backed beast. You know . . . (*Nudge, nudge.*) Two backs, four legs, four arms, two heads . . .

IAN   Are you sure you've got this right?

BILL   Yes . . . you know . . .

IAN   How many livers has it got?

BILL   Oh God . . . forget it . . .

IAN	I can't forget it now you've told me about it. And I've watched all the David Attenboroughs. It's got two backs . . . How many hearts?
BILL	Two, but only one brain. And only one set of genitals by the sound of things.
IAN	Ah, now we're getting somewhere. Does it have sex?
BILL	That's all it sodding does! The two-backed beast . . . it's two people. Surely you've heard this before? Two people having sex.
IAN	In my room?
BILL	Let me put this another way. Have you nobbed her? That's all I wanted to know. You don't have to say yes or no even, you just maybe smile in a certain way or make some sort of obscure remark and I'll understand, and I'll be happy, and we can talk about something else. Ok?
IAN	Why do you have to be so roundabout about it? If there's something you want to know just ask me. We're friends, I'll tell you.
BILL	Have you had sexual intercourse with Birgitta, the German rep you've been trailing around after for the last two weeks?
IAN	Mind your own business.
BILL	You haven't. Ok. Let's talk about something else.

(MONICA *returns, looking at her watch.*)

| MONICA | What have you done with Birgitta then, Ian? |
| IAN | Don't you start. You're sex mad, you two. |

(*There is a knock at the door.*)

| BILL | Aha! |

(BILL *goes to answer the door.*)

| IAN | Actually I suppose you could say I'm on a promise. |

BILL   Wooooh!

(BILL *shows* BIRGITTA *into the room. She is German, blonde and attractive. She is dressed in casual holiday gear - not her red rep's outfit as referred to above and later - she is tanned, and has brought some beer, which* BILL *takes care of.*)

BILL   Come in, Birgitta. Did you find it ok?

BIRGITTA   Oh yes. Hello everyone. Hello Ian.

(BIRGITTA *kisses* IAN *on the cheek.* BILL *and* MONICA *exchange a look as though this is a clue to how* IAN *and* BIRGITTA *are getting along.*)

BILL   You sit here, then, Birgitta.

MONICA   Drink?

IAN   Ooh yes, git a beer for Birgitta.

MONICA   Ian, has it ever occurred to you that a joke that is not funny remains not funny however often you repeat it? It becomes even less funny, in fact. Then it quite rapidly becomes extremely irritating.

IAN   Who rattled your cage?

BIRGITTA   I am not so sure. I have heard this joke by Ian eleven or twelve times, and it is beginning finally to become a kind of epic. The poor quality of the joke is making heroic the persistent telling of it.

BILL   I love it when you talk dirty. You speak like a character in an Anthony Trollope novel.

BIRGITTA   Oh, Barchester Towers is my third favourite novel.

MONICA   Why don't *you* get Birgitta a drink, Ian?

IAN   I'm just nicely settled now. Have you got any tea?

MONICA   This isn't a hotel, you . . . (*She realises, laughs, relaxes a little.*) No, there's no tea. This hotel is too expensive to have facilities.

IAN	I've got a kettle in my new room. I was very pleased when I saw that.
BILL	Have you bought coffee and stuff?
IAN	No point.
BILL	No, it's only one more day, isn't it?
IAN	No, there's no point in the room to plug it into.
BILL	Some wine, Birgitta?
MONICA	We haven't got any.
BILL	We can get some on room service.
MONICA	It'll be expensive.
BILL	What the hell. It's the World Cup semi-final. Champagne!

(BILL *moves to the phone and rings wine waiter*.)

IAN	I was telling Bill about the bathroom in my room. It's only about this big. The sink's here, right . . .
MONICA	You were telling me about it as well.
IAN	Yes, but Birgitta hasn't heard it yet. You see . . . (MONICA *exits to the balcony*.) . . . the sink's here, and the toilet's here, right underneath it, and the pipe from the plughole goes right into the toilet . . .
BIRGITTA	It sounds as if your room is - how do you say in English? It begins "cr . . . "
IAN	Cramped.
BIRGITTA	Craphole. That's it. Colloquial English, by W D Harmsworth. Crap is shit, I think.
IAN	Um, yes.
BIRGITTA	Thus I could say, "the dog took a crap".
IAN	No, no. It wouldn't take it. It might sniff it. It wouldn't take it.

(BILL *has finished his phone call and drifts back into the conversation.*)

BILL   Take a crap is American.

BIRGITTA   Aha, but we can also use it metaphorically, I think. Mrs Thatcher is crap.

BILL   Yes.

BIRGITTA   England are crap in football.

BILL   England are crap *at* football.

BIRGITTA   This is why Germany will win. You want to bet?

BILL   No, no more betting.

BIRGITTA   Cigarette, Bill?

BILL   Ah, Prince . . . (*He takes it. She offers him a light.*) No thanks, I'll stick it behind my ear.

BIRGITTA   It is no use there. If you wish to inhale you will need to be putting it in your mouth. Ah!

BILL   What's the matter?

BIRGITTA   Is this correct? "You will need to be putting it in your mouth"?

BILL   Er, yes, I suppose it is.

(BIRGITTA *claps.*)

BIRGITTA   This is my first ever spontaneous use of the future continuous infinitive.

BILL   Congratulations.

BIRGITTA   It is very helpful to speak with English people. Perhaps soon I will use a future perfect continuous.

BILL   Which is?

BIRGITTA   Will have been doing. So, at the end of this year, I will have been studying English for ten years.

BILL	By quarter past nine, England will have been scoring a goal every five minutes for an hour.
BIRGITTA	Very good. Soon you will have been speaking English like a native.
BILL	Yeah, like a native German.

(BILL *and* BIRGITTA *both laugh.* IAN *feels left out.*)

IAN	Do you fancy Birgitta or something, Bill?
BILL	What?
IAN	Anyway, as I was saying before I was so rudely interrupted. The sink's here, right, and the pipe from the sink goes straight into the toilet.

(BILL *shakes his head and joins* MONICA *on the balcony.*)

BILL	(*on the balcony*) He's doing his plumbing routine.
MONICA	Yes.
BILL	It's still a lovely view.
MONICA	Yes.
BILL	I love it when it's just getting dark.
MONICA	Hmmm.
BILL	It would be just right with a cigarette. Shame we don't face west. I think that was an extra tenner a night. Room with sunset.
MONICA	So you've said.
BILL	What would annoy me, if I had "room with sunset" is that someone could go out and sit on a rock and get one for free. A really good hotel would block out every possible sunset view on the island except the hotel's.
MONICA	My favourite bit is when all the lights come on. It's so sudden. The darkness sort of slinks in slowly . . .
BILL	It encroaches . . .

MONICA   Horrible word. Age encroaches, doesn't it? Lights
          come on. (*She laughs to herself.*) So have I, by the
          way.

BILL   Have you?

MONICA   Yes.

BILL   I was sort of hoping you might not.

MONICA   Yes I know.

BILL   It hasn't gone very well, this holiday, has it?

MONICA   No, not terribly.

BILL   England have been doing well.

MONICA   Yes.

BILL   Listen, who's fault is it, do you think?

MONICA   Rudi Gullit for not scoring against them.

BILL   You know what I mean.

MONICA   It's Ian's fault.

BILL   Oh come on . . . Ian's not the crime, he's the alibi.

MONICA   You realise that doesn't mean anything.

          (BILL *tries to think whether it means anything or not.*)

MONICA   I came on . . . came on this holiday in good faith. I
          hoped it would all be different, but, I don't know. It's
          the same match in a different stadium.

BILL   David Platt has really come on, hasn't he?

MONICA   I wonder if Ian has come on to Birgitta.

BILL   Do you remember when I first came on to you?

MONICA   (*laughs*) Yes.

BILL   You did, too.

MONICA   What?

BILL   Snore. I enjoyed it. It was so loud.

MONICA   Like a wildebeest with a drink problem.

BILL   No, it was wonderful. It was like a symphony for
              nose and throat.

              (*She laughs, the tension breaks. They embrace.* BILL
              checks his watch.)

MONICA   Bill?

BILL   What?

              (*She is about to say something but she suddenly
              looks up.*)

MONICA   The telephone's going to ring.

              (*Lights up on* BIRGITTA *and* IAN *in the room. She is
              laughing.*)

IAN   . . . I couldn't think of anything else that begins with
              'Sh' that I could do or I'd have done it.

BIRGITTA   Ian, you are such a funny little man. I know, you
              could have had a shag. Shag, another colloquialism.

IAN   (*taken aback*) Shag?

BIRGITTA   You have a shag, of course, when you are randy, I
              think.

IAN   Well, not absolutely every time . . . hardly ever . . .
              Birgitta?

              (*The phone rings.*)

BIRGITTA   Yes?

IAN   (*very quickly*) I just wanted to say . . . you're really
              nice . . . and I'm going home tomorrow and . . . Bill?
              Phone!

              (BIRGITTA *is a bit puzzled.* BILL *comes in from the
              balcony,* MONICA *comes to the edge of the room to
              see who's on the phone.*)

BILL   You could have answered it. It's probably room
            service.

IAN   No, no, your phone, not mine.

BILL   Hallo? Dan! Hallo Dan! Where are you calling from?
            No! Really? I thought you were in Burma . . . Hang
            on, hang on, I'll take you in the other room . . . oh
            yes, quite a flash hotel . . .

            (*He hangs up, and goes out to speak to* DAN *on the
            other phone. To* MONICA, *on his way out.*) Dan
            Hudson. (*Shrugs, and exits.* MONICA *reacts a little.*
            IAN *pretends not to know who* DAN *is.*)

IAN   Monica? Who is Dan Hudson, may we know?

MONICA   He's one of Bill's authors . . . (*Under her breath.*) . . .
            if it's any of your fucking business . . . surely Bill
            must have spoken about him? The train spotter.
            (*She leaves, returning to the balcony.*)

BIRGITTA   That was a bit nosey, wasn't it?

IAN   What was?

BIRGITTA   Asking about Bill's telephone call.

IAN   Perfectly civil question.

BIRGITTA   Nosey, nosey, nosey. Such an excellent word. I
            learnt it from a four year old girl the other day. I
            asked her what was her name, and she said to me
            "Don't be so nosey". She told me a joke, want to
            hear it? (IAN *nods.*) Knock knock.

IAN   Who's there?

BIRGITTA   Nigel.

IAN   Nigel who?

BIRGITTA   Nigel the monkey.

            (IAN *doesn't seem to get it, then somehow forces a
            laugh out. It is rather ghastly.*)

            It is just nonsense, that's what I like.

IAN	Birgitta . . . ? Your English is really good, isn't it?
BIRGITTA	Thank you.
IAN	What I was going to say is . . . you know I haven't got a job at the moment . . .
BIRGITTA	That's right. You used to work in Bill's company, didn't you?
IAN	Well, it's not his company, actually, Tate Publishing. It's quite a big firm.
BIRGITTA	So why did you leave?
IAN	It was quite funny actually. My office was just above the lobby, Ok? And just outside the window there was like a flat roof, and stuck on the front edge of this roof were big letters saying "TATE PUBLISHING". They lit up at night and everything. Well one afternoon I climbed out, crawled across the roof and pulled the "E" off. So it said 'TAT'. Tat Publishing. Pretty funny, eh?
BIRGITTA	Tat? This means something?
IAN	Yeah, it's like "crap". Crap Publishing.
BIRGITTA	The dog took a tat.
IAN	Ah, no . . .
BIRGITTA	England are tat at football.
IAN	Well, maybe . . .
BIRGITTA	Your room is a tathole. Tat Publishing, I see. Ha ha ha. Very funny, I like this. And so they sacked you?
IAN	Well not straight away. They sacked Bill first, because I hid this big neon "E" behind his filing cabinet, but then after a couple of days they found out it was me.
BIRGITTA	Well you told them, of course?
IAN	No . . . well, I would have done, obviously, Bill's my friend.

(*Small pause.* BILL *comes back from the phone.*)

BILL   Well kids, looks like there's going to be another mouth to feed. That was Dan Hudson, the Train Spotter. God knows what he's doing here. He's coming over to watch the game. Monica . . . ?

(BILL *wanders through to see where* MONICA *is.*)

IAN   Oh great! A gooseberry!

BIRGITTA   What?

IAN   Um . . . nothing. Anyway, what I was going to say . . . there's a good chance I could get another job soon, and I thought, your English is so good you'd easily fit in, and . . .

BIRGITTA   So this Dan Hudson is a train spotter?

IAN   Well he's written a book called "The Train Spotter". In England you see they're a bit of a joke, really. Often you see comedians pretending to be one, with an anorak on, and flared trousers, and a tank top, and big thick glasses with sellotape on and they talk like this . . . (*He gets up to do his train spotter, with a wanky adenoidal voice.*) Hullo, I'm a train spotter . . .

(MONICA *and* BILL *come back in.*)

MONICA   What on earth do you think you're doing?

IAN   Oh, I'm explaining to our German friend what a train spotter is. They don't have them.

MONICA   We couldn't move to Germany, could we?

BILL   Sixteen minutes. Actually, you know . . . I think I might just nip down and get some more beer.

MONICA   Oh Bill, there's plenty.

BILL   Yes, but Dan Hudson's coming. He's a fantastic drinker. I remember once he turned up for a meeting straight from a lunch where they'd had thirteen bottles of wine between five people.

MONICA   So?

BILL   Three of them weren't drinking.

MONICA   Ah.

BILL   (*looking at his watch again*) It won't take a minute. Come on, Ian, come and give us a hand.

IAN   Oh, ok.

            (BILL *and* IAN *leave. There is a slightly awkward pause.*)

BIRGITTA   So. Your holiday is almost over.

MONICA   That's right.

BIRGITTA   I will be sorry to see you go. You have been good company.

MONICA   What will you do? Find another group of English people to pal around with? Or maybe you could try Italians next time, or Americans?

BIRGITTA   Maybe. The English are really my favorite. They speak English so well. Almost as well as the Dutch. Bill has been especially good for me. He is so particular.

MONICA   How did the lesson go last night?

BIRGITTA   I'm sorry?

MONICA   You and Bill seemed to be talking for a long time last night.

BIRGITTA   Yes, well, you know, he was talking about football. He bet me he could name the 1975 Bayern Munich team. He got ten of them, but then he tried to claim that the left back was called Wiener Schnitzel.

MONICA   How do you know so much about football?

BIRGITTA   It is a bit embarrassing. When I was a girl I used to have a crush on Kevin Keegan. He played in Germany for Hamburg. I saw him once in a supermarket.

MONICA   Presumably buying up their stocks of hair spray.

BIRGITTA   Then later I had a boyfriend who was "ausgeflip" for
            football. (*She illustrates with a dramatic gesture.*)

MONICA   Ah yes, "ausgeflip" for football.

BIRGITTA   Too much. I said to him one day, "It's me or
            football". He chose me, but I finished with him
            anyway. He was no fun without the football.

MONICA   Bill said you were talking about Ian.

BIRGITTA   Oh yes - so many funny stories about Ian . . .

MONICA   I can imagine.

BIRGITTA   And about Bill's trouble at work - well, you know
            about that, of course.

MONICA   Do I? What trouble at work?

BIRGITTA   He worries that the company will fail, that he may
            lose his job, you know . . . (*Realises that* MONICA
            doesn't know.) It's not important. Maybe it was the
            tequila speaking.

MONICA   Maybe. Still, you were dancing together for a long
            time. Ian was getting quite restless. I think he thought
            you and Bill were going to run off together.

BIRGITTA   He's a very attractive man.

MONICA   Ian?!

BIRGITTA   No, Bill.

MONICA   Yes. Yes, I suppose he is.

BIRGITTA   And Ian too, in a way.

            (MONICA *gawps at her.*)

MONICA   What's German for "optician"?

BIRGITTA   No, seriously. I have found that the more socially
            inept the man, the better he is in bed.

MONICA   Really? I'd have thought the more socially inept a
            man is, the less likely you are to find out whether
            he's good in bed or not.

BIRGITTA   That's true, I suppose.

MONICA   How socially "ept" is Bill, do you think?

            (*Pause.*)

BIRGITTA   I'm looking forward to the game, aren't you? Who do
            you think will win?

MONICA   For heaven's sake, Birgitta, can't you and I talk about
            something other than football?

BIRGITTA   Ok. Why don't you show me the view from your
            balcony?

            (*She goes out to the balcony.* MONICA *follows. The
            lights rise on the hotel bar.* IAN *is sitting at the bar
            waiting for* BILL, *who is making a phone call. He has
            got himself a margherita with a little paper umbrella in
            it. Beside him on the bar are some more four-packs
            of San Miguel.* BILL *enters. He seems a bit edgy and
            distracted.*)

BILL   Ah, you got it, good. Good. How much do I owe you?

IAN   Oh that's alright . . .

BILL   Oh, thanks. (*He puts his wallet away.*)

IAN   I got them to put it on your bill.

BILL   Come on then, let's go.

IAN   Hang on, hang on. I haven't finished this yet.

            (BILL *sits on a stool to wait, looks at his watch.*)

            Everything alright?

BILL   Yeah, fine.

IAN   Get through ok?

BILL   Yeah. I was calling Geoff Tate, as a matter of fact.

IAN   Really? How is the humourless old so-and-so?

BILL   Well. He was giving me a lot of stick before we came away about letting Dan Hudson go off gallivanting around Burma without signing the contracts for his new book. I don't know, I tried everything to get in touch with him, I even put an ad in the Burmese Times, but nothing, no word or anything, and then the bastard turns up on my doorstep while I'm on holiday. Typical.

IAN   So was Tate pleased, then?

BILL   Hard to tell. I managed to make it sound like I'd found Hudson rather than him finding me, but still . . .

IAN   I expect he's just a bit jumpy about those rumours about a takeover.

BILL   How do you know about that?

IAN   I used to work there not so long ago, remember? You made a speech at my leaving do.

BILL   It was hardly a do. Half a bottle of Frascati in the photocopying room, and just the two of us . . .

IAN   It wasn't much of a speech, come to that.

BILL   Yes, well . . .

IAN   And you were only there for ten minutes.

BILL   I'm surprised I turned up at all.

IAN   Bill, I know I haven't apologised properly for that business . . .

BILL   Ian. Margherita. Mouth.

(Blackout on the bar. Lights rise on the balcony.)

BIRGITTA   No, none of my clients has a Mercedes. They are fairly low grade. My boys are not so different from the English. They are young. They have not come to Majorca to look at Robert Graves' house. They want the obvious things.

MONICA   Sun, sand, sex . . .

BIRGITTA   Drink, violence, and if the weather is not so good
              perhaps a little light shoplifting.

MONICA   You're very cynical.

BIRGITTA   Yes. I'm throwing in the towel at the end of this
              season. I'm going to settle in Berlin. To teach
              English, I hope.

MONICA   Berlin . . . that must be an exciting place to be just
              now.

BIRGITTA   It was before.

MONICA   You know what I mean. The wall coming down . . .

BIRGITTA   Yes, and all those East Germans rushing around
              everywhere. I have found it is very easy to spot the
              East Germans. Most of them look like Kevin Keegan.

MONICA   I thought we said no football.

              (*Pause.*)

BIRGITTA   It must be difficult to live with Bill and hate football.

MONICA   I don't hate football, of course I don't. I used to go to
              matches with Bill, and enjoyed it. Sometimes. I'll tell
              you what I really liked. The shouting. I really liked
              the shouting. When Spurs scored you could just
              shout at the top of your voice. (*Suddenly shouting at
              the top of her voice.*) Yaaaaaaaagh! (*Then, to*
              BIRGITTA.) I'm sure it's really good for you, actually,
              I feel better already. (*She shouts again.*) Yaaaaaagh!

BIRGITTA   (*amused, joining in*) Yaaaaaagh!

              (*A voice, possibly Swedish, is heard from the balcony
              below.*)

MAN'S   Hello girls! We are Swedish and we'd like to join
VOICE   your party!

BIRGITTA   What's the matter with you? The football's about to
              start. What are you, a man or a squirrel?

MONICA	Mouse.
BIRGITTA	A mouse or a squirrel. Stupid man.
MONICA	I sometimes think things would be much better if there were no men, don't you?
BIRGITTA	No.
MONICA	No.

(*Back down to the hotel bar.* BILL *is getting impatient to be back in the room.*)

IAN	Did you hear that?
BILL	What?
IAN	That shouting?
BILL	It's not the game starting, is it? (*Checks his watch.*) No, nine minutes yet. Come on Ian, for God's sake.
IAN	I'm coming, I'm coming. You can't just knock this stuff back, you know. It's really cold. It'll give me neuralgia.
BILL	Leave it, then.
IAN	Oh no, I'm not leaving it. I've already sent one back. The glass had salt all round the top. Can you believe it?
BILL	Look, you do what you like. I'm going back up . . .
IAN	No, Bill, wait a minute, wait a minute. There's something I wanted to ask you. It doesn't matter if you miss the beginning, does it?
BILL	(*incredulous*) What?!
IAN	Now look. While we're on our own, chaps together, away from the ladies . . . sit down, come on . . .
BILL	Oh, not now, Ian . . .
IAN	Put those down . . .

(*He takes the beer off* BILL *and puts it back on the bar.* BILL *heaves a heavy sigh and perches on a stool, looks at his watch again.*)

BILL   This better be good.

IAN   Now then. How long have we been friends?

BILL   Alright, how much do you want?

IAN   (*pretend hurt*) Bill! Listen. You like Birgitta, don't you?

BILL   Yes, I like her. Can I go now?

IAN   No, no, wait . . .You like her a lot, don't you?

BILL   She's a lovely girl.

IAN   And you'll miss her, when we go back to England, won't you?

BILL   Oh, I don't know, yes, probably . . . I'll send her a Christmas card. Can't we talk about this tomorrow?

IAN   What I'm thinking, you see, is this . . . Why don't you invite Birgitta to stay with you in England?

BILL   Eh?

IAN   Then, you see, I could just . . . sort of pop round . . . you know . . . Accidentally, kind of thing, and, er . . .

BILL   Oh, look, I don't know that Monica would go for that.

IAN   You don't have to ask her before you do anything, do you? I mean, just drop an invitation into the conversation, casually. She can't say no, then, can she?

BILL   Ian. Ask me about this another time. Tomorrow. We'll talk about this tomorrow.

IAN   It'll be too late then.

BILL   It's the World Cup semi-final in . . . (*Checks his watch.*) . . . seven and a half minutes . . . I'm going up. See you up there.

(BILL *grabs the cartons of beer and exits hurriedly.*)

IAN   Yes. Thanks. Thanks a lot.

(*He sips his margherita in a sulky fashion. Blackout on the bar. Lights rise in the room as* BIRGITTA *and* MONICA *re-enter from the balcony.*)

BIRGITTA   It was a very interesting dance. I'll show you . . .

(*She moves* BILL'S *chair back to give herself room.*)

MONICA   Oh, careful, don't muck about with Bill's seating plan. (*She moves the chair back to approximately where it was before.* BIRGITTA *looks puzzled.*) Everything has to be exactly right, exactly as it was when we watched the England-Cameroon game . . . is that it?

(BIRGITTA *shrugs. They grin naughtily.*)

Near enough.

(MONICA *leads* BIRGITTA *away from the chairs.*)

Now then, this dancing . . .?

BIRGITTA   Yes. He has copied Roger Milla . . .

MONICA   King of the Road.

BIRGITTA   What?

MONICA   Roger Miller, King of the Road. It's a song, he's a singer.

BIRGITTA   Not the same Roger Milla, the Cameroon player?

MONICA   No, no, no. But whenever Bill talks about that Roger Milla I say "Not, King of the Road?" It really pisses him off . . .

(*They laugh, an easy, unforced laugh.*)

BIRGITTA   Ok, so he is dancing along like he does, like a man trying to evacuate scorpions from his shirt . . .

(*She imitates* BILL'S *dancing, to* MONICA'S *approval.*)

MONICA   That's very good, actually . . .

BIRGITTA   And then, suddenly, he will come up to me and do
            this . . . (*She does the "Roger Milla" dance.*) . . . like
            Roger Milla when he has scored a goal.

MONICA   Let's have a go, show me again.

            (*They both do it.* BILL *comes in rather out of breath,
            and they stop guiltily.*)

BILL   What are you two up to?

MONICA   Nothing, nothing.

BILL   Dan not here yet?

MONICA   No.

BILL   He's cutting it a bit fine, isn't he?

            (*He heads for the kitchenette area with the beer. On
            his way, he notices that his chair has been shifted.
            Puts down the beer on the sideboard and
            painstakingly finds its proper position. Picks up the
            beer, and leaves the room.* MONICA *and* BIRGITTA
            are amused.)

MONICA   You haven't lost Ian, have you?

BILL   (*off*) No, he's coming.

MONICA   Only I wouldn't like to think of him wandering too
            near the edge of the pool, or out into heavy traffic,
            or along any crumbling cliff tops . . .

BILL   (*coming back in*) Yeah, yeah . . . Five minutes, twenty
            seconds. God he's left it late enough. Right, crucial
            moment. Telly on.

            (*He turns the telly on.* IAN *returns.*)

            Sound down. Take your seats. Good luck everybody.

            (*Shakes hands with everybody.*)

            Good luck, Birgitta.

BIRGITTA   Imperative subjunctive: may the best team win.

BILL   Certainly not. May England win. Good luck Ian.

IAN   I'll probably read actually . . . (*Looking at* BIRGITTA.)
              . . . or go for a walk.

MONICA   Deya's only sixty miles away.

BILL   Good luck Monica.

              (*We hear a klaxon offstage.*)

MONICA   I'll need it. That'll be Dan.

BILL   That'll be Dan. Thank God.

              (BILL *goes to answer the door.*)

BIRGITTA   I have never met anyone called Dan. He must be
              good at judo.

IAN   Eh?

BIRGITTA   First Dan. (*She laughs at her own joke.*) Is that as bad
              a joke in English as I think it is in German?

MONICA   Worse, possibly.

BIRGITTA   Oh well.

              (DAN *rushes into the room singing "ENG-ER-LAND!
              ENG-ER-LAND! ENG-ER-LAND" at the top of his
              voice and to the tune football supporters use to sing
              "Here we go, here we go, here we go . . . ". He is
              wet in swimming trunks carrying a plastic bag full of
              clothes and the klaxon we've already heard. Also he
              has a fluffy elephant toy under one arm. He runs past*
              BILL *into the room, round the assembled company
              and over to the balcony. Holds elephant up.*)

DAN   I bought this at the airport. God knows why. I must
              be losing my mind.

              (*He boots it off the balcony.*)

              West Germany nil, Stoke City six. Yes! (*Goes over to*
              MONICA.) Hello . . . Vanessa, isn't it?

BILL   Monica.

DAN	Monica. (*Sniffs.*) You've been eating pickled onions.
BILL	Have you been in the pool?
DAN	Couldn't resist it, mate. The pool in my hotel's full of fucking Germans.

(IAN *thrusts his hand out to introduce himself before* DAN *recognises him. A flicker of puzzlement passes across* DAN'S *face.*)

IAN	Ian Marshall. This is Birgitta. She's a fucking German.
DAN	Hello Birgitta. Dan Hudson . . . sorry . . .
BIRGITTA	Pleased to meet you, Dan. You're probably staying at my hotel, it's full of fucking Germans, I can't stand the place.

(*They laugh together and nobody is embarrassed except* IAN *on* BIRGITTA'S *behalf.* BIRGITTA *sits down.*)

DAN	The Bon Vista or something, it's called.
BIRGITTA	That's the one.
DAN	What a dump!

(DAN *sits down beside* BIRGITTA, *to* IAN'S *annoyance.*)

BILL	So. Argentina in the final, then?
DAN	Touch wood . . . (*Taps table.*) Is this wood, this thing?
BILL	That Maradona's a lucky bastard, isn't he?
DAN	Did you see his handball against Russia?
BILL	Yeah, just punched it off the line.
DAN	I don't know why they don't just put him in goal and have done with it.
BILL	Poor old Scotland, eh?

(*Pause, then* BILL *and* DAN *laugh triumphantly at Scotland's expense.*)

DAN   Same old story, though.

BILL   Yeah. The trouble with the Scotland team is that
           they're good on paper . . .

DAN   Shit on grass.

BILL   Shit on paper.

DAN   You saw Platt's goal?

BILL   God, yes, and everybody piled on top of him. Did
           you see Lineker's face? (*Does Lineker's open-
           mouthed rapture, as seen after Platt's goal against
           Belgium.*)

DAN   He couldn't believe it, could he?

BILL   And the Cameroons? They were brilliant. What a
           great player, Roger Milla . . .

BIRGITTA   King of the Road.

           (MONICA *grins.* DAN *is amused also, with* BIRGITTA.)

BILL   Hey, I've managed to play a bit too, since we've
           been out here.

DAN   Did you notch?

BILL   Got a hat-trick.

MONICA   What he hasn't mentioned, of course, is that it was on
           the beach, it was three a side, none of the other
           players was more than about nine, and the final score
           was twenty four-all. He looked like their dad.

           (*Pause.*)

BILL   One of them was a volley.

DAN   Really?

BILL   It's going to start in a minute. Sit down Ian, for God's
           sake . . .

IAN   I can't, actually. (*Makes a wanky gesture to indicate*
           DAN *is in his place.*)

DAN   Have I taken your seat, mate? Here . . . (*Getting up.*)

IAN   No, it's all wet now, you'd better stay there. It's ok, I
            like standing up.

MONICA   There's a stool in the bathroom.

BILL   Well it's not one of . . .

MONICA   No Bill . . .

BILL   Oh look, look! Here it comes! They do close-ups of .
            all the players, and get them to say their own names,
            and when it gets to Gascoigne he says "fucking
            wanker", he does, watch!

            (DAN *and* BILL *join in as the players do this.*)

BILL⎫   Mark Wright . . . Des Walker . . . David
DAN⎭   Platt . . . Fucking Wanker . . .

IAN   Is that witty, actually?

DAN   No. It's very self aware, though . . .

IAN   Because the thing you notice about Paul Gascoigne
            . . . Gazza . . . is that they all say what fun he is and
            what a great joker he is, but when they try and pin
            down exactly what it is he's done that's so amazingly
            funny it's always something like, oh, he threw
            somebody in a pool, or, oh, he pushed a cake in
            somebody's face, or, oh, he's thrown somebody else
            in the pool, I mean, really . . .

DAN   Oh, here come your lot, Birgitta. Any jokers in the
            pack?

BIRGITTA   Of course not, they are all Germans.

DAN   Fair point, well made.

BIRGITTA   In Munich in 1974 we had a player called
            Holzenbein, which in English means "wooden leg".

            (DAN *smiles at this.*)

MONICA   So what brings you to Majorca, Dan?

DAN   Bit of a busman's holiday, actually.

MONICA   Really?

DAN   There are drawbacks, obviously. I have to share a
              room with the busman's wife, and take the busman's
              kids to the beach and buy them ice cream . . .

              (BILL *and* MONICA *smile at this.*)

IAN   Ah, now, Birgitta, this is an English expression. In
              olden days, you see, the omnibus driver, or
              "busman" would always take his holidays . . .

MONICA   Oh do shut up, Ian.

BILL   Yes, shut up and sit down.

DAN   I'll explain it to you sometime, Birgitta.

BIRGITTA   Okay . . .

MONICA   So. What brings you to Majorca then, Dan?

DAN   There's a line from Palma to Soller across the island.
              Thought I might do a piece on it, you know . . . (*He's
              not very convincing.*)

BILL   What, that little . . . ? I mean it's only a little half hour
              tourist run, I wouldn't have thought it was your style.
              I thought you were doing the Rangoon to Mandalay
              line.

DAN   It's my book. What do you care as long as it sells?

BILL   Absolutely right, you're the boss. No, hang on, I'm
              the boss, but you're still absolutely right.

DAN   Anyway the football angle's better. Burma didn't
              even enter the World Cup. At least you can bump
              into footballers on Majorca. Did you know Graeme
              Souness is staying in your hotel?

BILL   Is he?

IAN   Who is Graeme Souness please?

BIRGITTA   The manager of Glasgow Rangers.

DAN   (*impressed*) Very good. Yeah, bumped into him in the
             lobby, and he apologised to me. Calls himself a hard
             man, coh!

             (DAN *gets up to put his trousers on. While he is
             standing up* IAN *sidles over and sits next to* BIRGITTA
             again.)

BILL   Here we go . . . (*He looks at his watch so he has the
             exact kick-off time.*)

DAN   Shall I shut the curtains?

BILL   If you want.

MONICA   No, it'll be too dark.

             (MONICA *goes out to the balcony.* DAN *squashes in
             between* IAN *and* BIRGITTA. IAN *is uncomfortable.*)

DAN   Right. Here we go.

             (*The game starts. In the room* BILL, DAN, IAN *and*
             BIRGITTA *watch with varying degrees of intensity.*
             MONICA'S *monologue is punctuated by anguished
             "oooh!" noises as England come close in early
             stages.*)

MONICA   (*on the balcony, looking out*) I shall never forget the
             first words Gary Lineker said to me. "So, you're the
             Monica everyone's been talking about . . . " I should
             say they were the *first* first words he said to me.
             The second first time we met he said: "Is it possible,
             sweet lady, for your laugh to be as beautiful as your
             eyes . . . ?"

             (*In the room the others go "Ooooooh!" at some bit of
             football.*)

             When I met him in the hotel I couldn't believe what
             he said. He emerged from the swimming pool,
             athletically of course, in one bound without touching
             the side . . . he strolled over to me and said: "My
             room is number 101, and if you come in half an hour
             I won't be surprised."

(In the room the others go "Aaaaaah!" at some bit of football.)

I was a little shocked at Gary saying that . . . but I went.

Dan. Dan Hudson's first words to me were . . .

(Flashback to DAN'S *book launch.* DAN *has moved into foreground, and we are in a bar, in a flashback, at a press launch for one of his books. He is on a stool, listening to a walkman.)*

DAN   Fucking bollocks to it! What a shagwanking disaster!

(He rips the headphones off and looks very dejected.)

MONICA   Are you all right?

DAN   Two bastard nil. Do you want a drink?

MONICA   Aren't you Dan Hudson?

DAN   Yes. Do you want a drink?

MONICA   It's next door.

DAN   Oh no, it's very much here. Do you want a drink?

MONICA   I've just left one. I only came in to use the loo.

DAN   *(to imaginary barman)* A bottle of brown ale by the neck for the lady, Terry.

MONICA   I thought you'd be at the book launch.

DAN   One person more or less won't make much difference.

MONICA   You did write the book.

DAN   I hate book launches. Book launches, Vanessa, are a waste of quiche.

MONICA   Why did you call me Vanessa?

DAN	I always guess women's names. It's a little game I have with myself. One day I'm going to get it right, and when I do I'm going to give the woman in question a weekend for two in Vienna. (*He pulls two tickets out of his pocket.*) I'll have to get one right soon, these run out in a month.
MONICA	Oh well . . . I'm afraid I'm Monica. I'm Bill's wife. Bill Desbackos.
DAN	Oh yes, Bill Desbackos. He's got a whole fleet of lorries now, hasn't he?
MONICA	Bill Desbackos. He works for your publishers.
DAN	Oh, Bill . . .
MONICA	I liked your book.
DAN	Did you read it?
MONICA	No.
DAN	Good. That's the best way to enjoy it.
	(MONICA *pulls one out of her bag.*)
MONICA	I can tell it's good, though, because of the blurb on the back.
DAN	You bought one?
MONICA	Free copy . . . (*Reads.*) . . . "The Train Spotter" by Dan S. Hudson. When he spots a train, he gets on it. How do you describe the majestic splendour of the Amazonian rain forests? Where can you marvel at the mighty temples of Atahualpa? And how do you find out the Stoke City score when you're 350 miles from the nearest phone and the local Indians all support Manchester United?
DAN	I hate that.
MONICA	I think it's rather funny.
DAN	It's crap, 'cos it makes it seem like South America is great and Stoke City are crap and boring.

MONICA   Is South America not great, then?

DAN   Oh yes, but it's no Stoke on Trent. And Stoke City
F.C. is the most important thing in my life.

(MONICA *laughs*.)

I'm serious.

MONICA   I'm sure you are. Would you miss your mother's
funeral for a game?

DAN   My mother would know not to get herself buried on
a Saturday afternoon. She loves me. She will die in
the close season. Will you spend an hour with me?

MONICA   Yes, all right.

DAN   What was your name again?

MONICA   Vanessa.

(*They look at each other for a long moment.
Meanwhile, in the room,* BILL *is watching an England
attack. He is forward on the edge of his seat. The
attack fails, and he lets out a long groan. He sits back
in his chair and looks towards the balcony.*)

BILL   Monica? Monica? Monica?

(MONICA *doesn't react, stays looking at* DAN. BILL
looks puzzled. Blackout. End of part one.)

Part Two

*From the darkness, the light from the television brightens to show
all five are in the room watching the game, in a tableau.* BILL *is
standing with his hands on the back of the chair, leaning forward.*
DAN *is squatting on the floor close to the television, his arms
wrapped tightly around his knees. They are deeply into the game.*
BIRGITTA *is watching the game, smoking a cigarette which she
holds near her mouth.* MONICA *sits looking at the ceiling.* IAN
*stands with his back to us, looking at one of the pictures on the
wall.*

After a few moments of this tableau, an English attack begins and the stage lights rise. DAN begins a crescendo of "Go on! Go on!" which culminates in a loud groan. He tips over and rolls around on the ground, hugging his knees even tighter. At the same time BILL goes "Yeeeeeeeeees! No!", and, as DAN rolls he turns away from the television and raises his eyes and arms to the heavens.
BIRGITTA, watching the game, brings her cigarette to her mouth slowly, and as the attack fails she inhales and smiles an enigmatic teutonic smile. MONICA brings her gaze down to the television in time to see the England miss. She can't help but do a soundless "Ooooooh!", then she looks away at the floor. IAN turns just too late to see the piece of action. He watches their reactions.

IAN   Is it still the first half?

(No one pays him any attention.)

I was thinking, it's bizarre really, isn't it? We're watching a football game which is happening in Italy, we're in Spain, and we're all English. Apart from Birgitta. She's German.

(Still nobody responds.)

Different cultures are really funny sometimes, aren't they? For instance I was up in Scotland once, and if you want to get fish and chips there you don't say fish and chips you have to say "fish supper". Even if it's lunchtime, fish supper. Or pie and chips, "pie supper". It's like "supper" means "and chips". I wanted to go in and say "chip supper, please", and see if I got two lots of chips. Or not. Anyway.

BILL
DAN   } Handball!

DAN   Surely!

BIRGITTA   No, no . . .

DAN   Referee!

BIRGITTA   What is the referee's name?

BILL   Jose Ramirez Wright.

BIRGITTA   Wright? That is the name of one of your players. Mark Wright.

BILL   He's Brazilian, the ref.

BIRGITTA   I don't think this is justice when the referee is the father of one of your team.

IAN   Is Mark Wright Brazilian, then . . . ?

DAN   Shut up, Ian.

IAN   Very nice. If you want my opinion . . .

BILL
DAN
BIRGITTA   }   Ooooooh!
MONICA

DAN   You've got to hand it to Shilton, haven't you.

BIRGITTA   What?

IAN   What?

BIRGITTA   What have you got to hand to Shilton?

DAN   It. If you've got it you've got to hand it to Shilton. It's the law.

BILL   Go on Gary . . . !

(Whatever Gary is trying fails. They register this.)

BIRGITTA   He is very quick, this Lineker.

IAN   Yes, this Lineker is very quick. The other one is very slow.

BIRGITTA   Du bist die Scheisse die Gary Lineker in seinem Arschloch hat.

MONICA   Hands off Gary, he's mine.

IAN   I don't know. What do women see in Gary Lineker, eh? I mean he's very boring, isn't he . . . .?

(Just for a moment, everyone forgets the game and stares at IAN. *Then they turn back.)*

DAN   Oh, Beardsley was wide, Beardsley was wide!

BIRGITTA   Beardsley was wide, but now he's gone on a diet.

DAN   Birgitta. You are an exciting and sexy woman. Please don't spoil it by making feeble jokes.

BIRGITTA   *(a bit taken aback)* You want me to be a funny Nazi? You like this kind of German? Then you must also accept that I have no sense of humour. Arschloch!

(DAN stands up and kisses her smartly on the mouth.)

DAN   I'm sorry.

(He sits again. A German attack is building up. BILL, IAN *and* MONICA *are still reacting to* DAN'S *kiss.* IAN *is horrified.* DAN *watches telly through his fingers.)*

IAN   You must get fed up with the stereotype, though, Birgitta. Germans have no sense of humour, let's see, they're also meticulous, efficient, blonde . . . *(Takes a chance.)* . . . randy?

MONICA   Randy? The Germans aren't randy. Scandinavians are randy.

IAN   Ah, now, I think you'll find that only your Swedes are randy. Norwegians aren't randy, it's too cold. And the Danish are . . . well, they eat a lot of pastries, don't they?

DAN   Is this your first time abroad, Ian?

IAN   Yes, actually.

MONICA   My point is that Germans aren't randy.

DAN   Are you randy, Birgitta?

BIRGITTA   What does randy mean?

(We should know she knows from earlier.)

MONICA   What are the English supposed to be like, Birgitta?

BIRGITTA   I learnt all about the English from the Robinsons.

MONICA   Who were they?

BIRGITTA   They were the family in "Let's Speak English With The Robinsons".

IAN   Letts? I didn't know they did language books, I thought they only did travel guides.

BIRGITTA   No, no, "Let *us* Speak English with the Robinsons".

IAN   Oh.

BIRGITTA   They were a typical English family. Mr Robinson, Mrs Robinson, and their son, Ringo. I used to draw lots of curly hair onto Ringo to make him look like Kevin Keegan. (MONICA *laughs*.) And sometimes a microphone in his hand, and a speech bubble singing "Head over Heels in Love".

MONICA   Oh God, yes, he had a record, didn't he?

    (BIRGITTA *starts to sing,* MONICA *tries to join in.*)

BIRGITTA   "It looks like I'm fallin' all over again . . . Head over Heels in Love . . ."

IAN   (*completely baffled*) What are you talking about?

BILL
DAN   } Shhhhhhhhh!

BILL   Oh, offside, Waddle, you fool!

IAN   Ah. Now there's something I never really got hold of. Offside. What goes on there, hmmm?

DAN   It's really very simple. The ball has to pitch in a line directly between the stumps and strike the batsman on the leg without or before hitting the bat, below the height of the stumps, and have been going to hit the stumps. Got it?

IAN   (*sarcastically, realising the piss is being taken*) Thank you.

DAN   Jesus, how long till half time?

BILL   (*checking watch*) We're in injury time.

DAN   Oh fuck, I can't wait. Where's the pisser, in there?

             (MONICA *gestures.* DAN *trots out.*)

IAN   Hey everybody, let's do that thing, you know, he'll
             have just, you know, got started, and we all shout
             "goal". After three. One, two, three . . . GOAL!

             (*No one else joins in this merry jape.*)

BIRGITTA   Monica and Bill. I suspect you believe Ian to be a . . .
             (*She thinks.*) . . . dozy pratt? Or a . . . pillock.

IAN   I don't think swearing is particularly funny, Birgitta,
             especially in a foreigner.

             (DAN *returns.*)

BILL   (*relaxing*) That's it, half time. 0-0.

DAN   Surely not. The shout of "goal!" led me to believe
             someone had scored. I've been kidded! What a
             chump I've been! Doooh!

             (DAN *slaps his own forehead and falls over.* BILL *gets
             up and goes towards the balcony.*)

BILL   Come and have a look at our expensive view, Dan. I
             want a word with you.

             (*He goes outside onto the balcony.* DAN *grimaces at*
             MONICA, *and follows.*)

BIRGITTA   What ever happened to that champagne . . . ? (*She
             settles for a beer.*)

             (*Lights go down on the room.* IAN *goes to the toilet.
             On the balcony,* DAN *joins* BILL.)

BILL   We're doing well, aren't we?

DAN   Not bad.

BILL   I can't believe you're here.

DAN   Yeah. I wanted to stay in Europe. Couldn't face
        Stoke. Then when I heard you were here, I thought
        there must be a piece I can do in Majorca. You
        know, lager louts and mountains . . .

BILL   Hate the mountains, love the lager louts.

DAN   That sort of thing.

BILL   I'm about to have my finest moment of the holiday.
        Sorry, Monica.

        (*He takes the cigarette from behind his ear, and a
        lighter from his pocket.* DAN *snatches the cigarette
        and chucks it off the balcony.* BILL *groans.*)

DAN   For your own good.

BILL   Yeah. Look. I know this isn't the best time to bring
        this up . . .

DAN   What?

BILL   You haven't signed the contract for your new book
        yet.

DAN   Contracts . . .

BILL   I heard a rumour that you met somebody from
        Hutchinsons.

DAN   Enough shop talk, I think. Who's this Birgitta? Where
        does she fit in?

BILL   We met her at a karaoke night at the Benny Hill bar.

DAN   (*winces*) The Benny Hill bar?

BILL   Honestly. It's between the Peter Sellers bar, and
        Leapy Lee's barbecue disco. She works for this
        holiday company, and she wears this bright red outfit,
        and Ian got up and sang "The Lady in Red" to her.

DAN   Ian did? (*Mimes sticking his fingers down his throat.*)

BILL   Yeah, she just sort of attached herself to us after that.
        I think she fancies you, you know.

DAN   Isn't she with Ian?

BILL   Well. "With", as Birgitta would probably say, is a flexible preposition. You play your cards right. I mean it is England versus West Germany.

DAN   Is that a dare?

BILL   If you like.

DAN   When I was a kid I was always doing stupid dares. At six I ate a live stag beetle.

BILL   (*disgusted*) Oh God!

DAN   I had to do it - it was a quadruple dare. When I was nine a girl dared me to bang my head against a wall until my head started bleeding. And when I started doing it she shouted: "Don't, Dan, I didn't mean it, I'll kiss you if you like." But I had to. It was a dare and I was the original Dan Dare. Always finish, even in practice.

BILL   All right then, I dare you. I bet you can't . . .

MONICA   (*calling from inside*) Bill?

           (DAN *laughs, and wanders back into the room.* MONICA *joins* BILL *on the balcony, worrying about the conversation between husband and lover, and* DAN'S *laughter perplexes her. In the room,* DAN *joins* BIRGITTA. IAN *is not there.*)

DAN   Birgitta . . . have they left you all on your own?

BIRGITTA   Ian has gone for a tat.

           (DAN *gets a beer.*)

           So you are a writer, then, Dan? You don't seem like a writer.

DAN   How does a writer seem?

BIRGITTA   Well you should have a pipe and a tweed jacket and perhaps a drink problem.

DAN   One out of three. I became a writer because I went
               to a football match. Flamenco v Boca Juniors in Rio
               de Janeiro. I missed the plane back and ended up
               staying for three months. Got back just in time for the
               first match of the new season against Ipswich - nil nil
               - and I had no money, no job and an ex-girlfriend
               had rented out my flat. Then someone asked me to
               write an article, and the article turned into another
               article, and then a book, and then a stupid television
               programme, and another book, and now I'm a
               fucking stupid cult.

BIRGITTA   You really are remarkable. Such a masterful
               command of colloquial English. Do you know the
               works of W. D. Harmsworth?

DAN   W. D.? Oh, yes. How to swear on six continents.
               Subtitle: seven if you count the fucking Antarctic.

               (BIRGITTA *gets this joke and laughs at it.*)

BIRGITTA   So tell me. Why did your girlfriend become 'ex'?

DAN   I went to a football match the day before our wedding.

BIRGITTA   So? That doesn't seem such a big deal.

DAN   It was Flamenco v Boca Juniors in Rio de Janeiro. [I
               missed the plane, ended up staying three months . . .]

               (BIRGITTA *laughs.* BILL *comes in from the balcony on
               his way to the toilet and meets* IAN, *coming back from
               the toilet.*)

IAN   I'd give it a couple of minutes if I were you.

               (BILL *risks it.* IAN *comes in and sits.* DAN *and*
               BIRGITTA *feel that their conversation cannot continue
               as a threesome, and there is silence for a moment or
               two. Then* DAN *jumps up and goes out to the
               balcony, seeing his chance to get* MONICA *on her
               own for a quick chat.*)

DAN   Excuse me, I think I'll just check on our hostess.

               (IAN *and* BIRGITTA *watch him go. Pause.*)

IAN   Shall I get you a beer, Birgitta?

             (*This time, even* BIRGITTA *is not particularly amused.
             She perhaps lights a cigarette, and we get the feeling
             that not much of a conversation happens in the room
             during the following balcony scene. Lights down on
             the room.* IAN *gets up and wanders around. As* DAN
             emerges onto the balcony, MONICA *is looking at the
             view yet again.*)

DAN   Monica, isn't it?

MONICA   Hello, Mr Hudson.

DAN   Oooh, aren't we formal . . .

MONICA   Don't tell me you'd rather talk to me than watch the
             game.

DAN   Half time. I didn't realise Bill was so into football.

MONICA   Didn't you?

DAN   No, well, you know, I don't really see him off-duty.

MONICA   He was always really serious about it, when I met
             him, and before I met him, but these last few months
             he's just really . . . I don't know . . . lost himself in it.
             It's like nothing is as important as the games.

DAN   Oh, yeah, big Spurs fan, isn't he . . .

MONICA   What with things going badly, at work and, well, you
             know . . .

DAN   (*looking over the edge*) Long way up. Long way
             down. Do you dare me to lean out?

             (*Before she can reply he has clambered over the
             rail.* MONICA *shrieks at him to get back.*)

MONICA   God Almighty! Get back here! Dan, please!

DAN   What do you dare me? One hand?

             (*She makes a grab for his nearest arm to keep hold
             of him but he lifts it up and she misses it. He hangs by
             one hand. She covers her face.*)

MONICA   Christ!

DAN   One finger?

MONICA   No!

DAN   Little finger?

(*He leans out with his little finger crooked over the rail.*)

MONICA   Oh fuck off and kill yourself, I don't care.

(MONICA *turns her back on him. He climbs silently back onto the balcony, then slides his foot quickly on the floor as if he has lost his footing and makes the fading cry of a man falling to his death.*)

DAN   Yaaaaaaaaargh!

(MONICA *screams, spins round and looks over the rail, appalled. In the room* IAN *hears this, and looks out to see what has happened. Realising she's been had, she turns to face* DAN, *slowly.*)

DAN   Don't care, eh?

(MONICA *punches him hard in the stomach.*)

DAN   OOOOOF! Fair point, well made. Oooof!

(*They embrace.* DAN *sees* IAN *peering at them and steers* MONICA *to the far end of the balcony away from his view.*)

MONICA   What do you think you're doing here, anyway?

DAN   You haven't told him yet, then?

(MONICA *turns and looks out at the sea.*)

Only when you rang me yesterday you said you were going to tell him . . .

MONICA   Does he look like I've told him?

DAN   How the hell do I know? People are strange with bad news, sometimes. Sometimes people get relentlessly cheerful. "Your family's been hacked to death." "Oh well, you've got to laugh, haven't you . . . " I don't know. I mean, he is English.

(*Pause.*)

Are you going to? Only I think you shouldn't.

MONICA   Is that why you came out here? To tell me that I shouldn't leave Bill?

DAN   Well . . . things are all right as they are, aren't they?

MONICA   Are they?

DAN   Aren't they? Afternoons . . . ? You know. My flat is a slum.

MONICA   (*with heavy irony*) Dan, take me away from all this.

DAN   I was afraid you were going to say something like this. Listen, Monica. We've played some terrific games together, some really entertaining fixtures. Four-all draws, with a sending off, and a dog on the pitch. It's been great, those afternoons, that weekend, Vienna, Vanessa . . . but . . . but, you know, I don't want us to get into the first division. We haven't got the stadium, we haven't got the facilities . . .

BILL   (*from inside*) You two all right out there? Two minutes to the start of the second half.

MONICA   It's so sad. You and Bill are exactly the same.

DAN   Don't tell him. He supports Spurs, he's got enough problems.

MONICA   I don't know how to talk to you. Dan, don't you realise we have to make decisions. It's not football. You have no control over the result of a football match . . .

DAN   Oh, if only I did. It would be the same every season. League Champions: Stoke City. F A Cup winners: Stoke City. Government: Stoke City. Prime minister: Jimmy Greenhoff . . .

MONICA   You sad fucker . . .

DAN   Well . . . Don't you have a fantasy?

MONICA   No.

BILL   (*calling*) Teams are coming out!

DAN   Second half.

             (DAN *trots back into the room, leaving her on the balcony.*)

MONICA   Of course what he's really worried about is the press finding out. "Lineker in Sordid Love-nest Scenario". They could use that to ruin his career. And his game would suffer, inevitably.

             So we go to extraordinary lengths to make sure nobody finds out about us. The secret rendezvous, the elaborate disguises. Me the blind match girl outside the Dorchester, he the visiting operatic tenor from Barcelona.

             I remember once he turned up on my doorstep with a huge industrial carpet cleaning machine, pretending to be my new home-help. Got the idea from an advert he was doing, he said.

             It's not just the publicity, though. Neither of us wants to hurt Bill . . . or Michelle, for that matter.

             And Gary's naturally very concerned about what the future holds. I think his biggest worry is that he'll turn into Jimmy Greaves. I'm quite worried about that too, as it happens . . .

             (IAN *joins* MONICA *on the balcony.*)

IAN   It is a rather splendid view, isn't it?

MONICA   We're paying thirty quid a week extra for that. If you're out here for more than a minute I'll have to start charging you.

IAN   Ha ha ha, charging me . . . charging me, that's a good one . . . yep . . . So how much did our friend Mr Hudson pay for the privilege?

MONICA   You what?

IAN   Just now . . . for the view . . .

            (MONICA *rolls her eyes upwards and tuts. They both
            look out. Back inside the room,* DAN, BILL *and*
            BIRGITTA *are watching the start of the second half.*
            BILL *is intent on the TV set.*)

BILL   OK, here we go. Forty five minutes and then we'll
            know, unless there's extra time. Forty five minutes
            and then we might know. Seventy five minutes and
            then we'll definitely know. Unless there's penalties.
            Ninety minutes, and then we'll definitely definitely
            know.

            (*Back on the balcony.*)

IAN   Look, it's the airport.

MONICA   I've seen it.

IAN   There, just there, look. Where the planes are going.

MONICA   There's plenty more beer inside, if you want some.

IAN   (*holding up a bottle to show her*) Got some.

MONICA   You're missing the game, aren't you?

IAN   (*shrugs*) Football.

            (MONICA *looks quizzically at him. She wants to be
            alone.*)

MONICA   Oh, wasn't that Birgitta calling you?

IAN   Naah, don't think so.

            (*In the room.*)

DAN   What do you reckon, Birgitta? Do you fancy your
            chances?

BIRGITTA   The English are playing well. I like their fluid
            defensive system, it looks very secure, and
            Gascoigne is controlling the midfield even though
            England are outnumbered there, but Germany are a

strong running side that combine well as a unit and I
think that as the game goes on England will tire and
Germany will take control.

DAN   Yes, but I wasn't talking about the game.

(*They share a flirty sort of look, which* BILL *is too
intent to notice. The focus shifts back to the balcony.*
MONICA *is losing patience.*)

MONICA   Well it's been lovely, but I think I'll go inside. It's
getting a bit chilly.

IAN   Don't go yet. I think you and I ought to have a little
chat.

MONICA   Do you? What about? Only that stuff about the
airport was just too exciting for me, I think I need a
bit of a lie down.

IAN   About my future.

MONICA   Your future. What's that got to do with me?

IAN   I've got this contact at Hutchinson's . . .

MONICA   Have you now? And if you get a job with them you'll
be in direct competition with Bill . . . so obviously
you won't be able to socialise with us quite so much,
in fact, not at all. Oh well, it'll be a wrench, at first, but
I think we'll survive . . .

IAN   I haven't got a job there . . . yet . . . but I could have
one if, for the sake of argument, I could take a well-
known author with me from Tate's.

MONICA   You don't work at Tate's any more.

IAN   I know.

MONICA   So what well-known author were you thinking of?

IAN   I was thinking of Dan Hudson, actually.

(MONICA *gapes at him. Back inside the room* DAN,
BILL *and* BIRGITTA *react to an incident on the screen.
Perhaps* DAN *has come and sat next to* BIRGITTA.)

DAN   Oooh you bugger!

BIRGITTA   That was close.

BILL   That could have been it . . . that could have been it . . .

DAN   I tell you the strain's going to get to me. I'll be
            knackered by the end of this.

BIRGITTA   Oh I hope not.

            (DAN *is momentarily surprised that she knows the
            word 'knackered', then they share another look.*)

BILL   (*to the television*) Go on you bastard, get in there!
            Get in there! Get in there!

            (*Back on the balcony,* IAN *and* MONICA *continue
            their discussion.*)

MONICA   You're bonkers! Dan'll never go for that, why should
            he?

IAN   I thought maybe you could have a word with him for
            me.

MONICA   Me? What makes you think he'll listen to me
            suggesting he should ruin my husband's career?

IAN   You tell me.

            (*Pause.*)

MONICA   I see. It's like that is it?

IAN   Looks like it.

MONICA   So Dan goes to Hutchinson's with you, or . . .

IAN   I'm Bill's friend.

MONICA   Some friend. You fuck him up both ways.

IAN   You know the travel publications business. It's dog
            eat cat out there.

            (*Pause.*)

MONICA   Something else?

IAN   No . . . I just thought you might say "That's blackmail" and then I could say "Blackmail's an ugly word, this is just business." But you're not going to, are you, so it doesn't matter.

MONICA   I ought to throw you over, you shit . . .

IAN   Oh, Brit in Balcony Death Plunge Horror, you mean? Nice one.

    (*Inside the room,* DAN *is leading* BILL *and* BIRGITTA *in the chant that football crowds do when a goalie is taking a goal kick.*)

DAN   Wooooooooooooooh! You're! Shit! Aaaaaaaaaagh!

    (IAN *goes into the room, and* DAN *continues going "Aaaaaagh!" much longer than the others, straight at* IAN, *who applauds.*)

IAN   Author! Author!

    (DAN *loses interest, and turns back to the telly.* MONICA *stays on the balcony.* BILL *talks out to audience.*)

BILL   During the game itself my mind was wandering. I kept trying to concentrate, to tell myself that this was the most important game for twenty four years, but I found thoughts popping into my head, about my garage, about a prawn cocktail I'd had the night before that had a particularly tough prawn right at the bottom and how I'd thought it might not actually be a prawn, and, ridiculously, I thought what if Dan being here wasn't an accident . . . ?

    And then Hassler, the little German midfielder goes down and it's a free kick on the edge of our area . . .

DAN   . . . and it's obviously a dive, just *obviously*, because he does that thing where you run on a couple of steps until you're absolutely sure that you've lost the ball and then he lets himself down carefully so he doesn't hurt himself, the little bastard . . .

IAN   Ooh, that looked like rather a bad tackle, actually . . .

             (DAN *glares at him.* MONICA *enters.*)

MONICA   Would anyone like me to get them anything?

BILL   (*irritable*) Not now, Monica, can't you see it's a free
             kick?

MONICA   Well maybe our guests would like something. Dan?

DAN   (*snaps*) Not now, Monica, it's a free kick.

             (MONICA *is somewhat put out by their manner.*)

IAN   Yes, could I have another bottle of San Miguel,
             please, Monica?

MONICA   Not now, Ian, can't you see it's a free kick?

             (*She becomes interested in the game suddenly.*)

BIRGITTA   I'll get you one. I want one too, in any case.

             (BIRGITTA *goes to get beer from the kitchenette.*)

IAN   Thank you, Birgitta. I think I might support Germany
             for a bit.

DAN   It's taken forever for the German to pick himself up
             and get on with the free kick. Brehme's the
             dangerous one, we've seen him score and come
             close several times in the tournament, and when they
             finally take the kick it's knocked to him and he
             shoots!

BILL   It's all right though, because Parker, the little centre
             half, he's run out and blocked it from a couple of
             yards away, it's gone right up in the air . . .

DAN   . . . easy for Shilton, that, easy except that . . . he's
             way out of his goal, he can't get back, he's on his
             arse, and it's gone in, I don't fucking believe it!

BILL   Germany score, and I think . . . it's my fault.

DAN   I don't fucking believe it!

MONICA   Germany score, and I think . . . yes, that'll teach you.

DAN   I don't fucking believe it!

IAN   Well, now, be fair. It was a good goal.

DAN   (*turning on him*) I don't fucking believe you! Where do you fucking come from? It was a bloody terrible goal! It was a fucking *own* goal by Shilton. Shilton . . . he's like a fucking wildebeest with a drink problem.

            (BIRGITTA *comes back with two beers.*)

BIRGITTA   Oh . . . did we score?

DAN   Yes you fucking scored.

IAN   Now look here. I don't mind you swearing at me . . .

DAN   Thank fuck for that you soft twat. Now shut your fucking dopy cunt mouth until you learn something about football.

            (*Pause.*)

BIRGITTA   Perhaps at this point it would be best if I apologise formally for being German.

IAN   Don't be daft. It's only a game after all.

DAN   You just feel so powerless, don't you.

MONICA   I thought that was the whole point. I thought the whole point was to abdicate responsibility.

BILL   Thank you Desmond Wilcox.

DAN   Go on, you . . . (*He groans with disappointment as a move breaks down.*)

BILL   We're going to lose, aren't we? I mean there's no way back from this . . .

BIRGITTA   Oh Bill, it's only one-nil.

IAN   Yes, come on Billy, chin up. It's not the end of the world.

DAN	Oh God, look, they've gone to pieces out there.
MONICA	Well. There's nothing you can do about it, is there.
BILL	What if . . . what if . . . Monica . . . what if there was something we could do about it? Eh?
MONICA	What do you mean?
BILL	That trick you used to do, that thing, you remember?
MONICA	You are joking, aren't you?
BILL	How do you know? You never really tried anything else, did you?
BIRGITTA	What's this? What are you talking about?
BILL	She's magic, our Monica is, she's psychic. She's a psychic phenomenon.
IAN	Really?
MONICA	Oh Bill . . . I used to be able to . . . it was just a little thing in the old days, I used to be able to make Bill think of me and ring me, if I wanted him to ring me. It wasn't anything really. I haven't done it for years.
BILL	She was on the telly.
MONICA	I was a tiny part of a documentary about the "mysteries of the mind" that went out at four in the morning on Harlech.
IAN	I see, so what you're thinking is if Monica can somehow communicate with the German goalkeeper, he'll want to ring her, and he'll leave the pitch immediately. Birgitta, quick, what's German for "telephone Monica at once".
BIRGITTA	(*irritated*) Oh Ian . . .
IAN	No it's a great plan. It could take him months to even find the number here.
DAN	Wide, you blind bastard!
BIRGITTA	So I don't understand. Bill, what do you want to try?

BILL   I don't know. Maybe for Monica to try and *will*
            England to score.

MONICA   You really are desperate, aren't you?

BILL   Monica, come on. Fifteen minutes to go, in the World
            Cup semi-final. What possible harm can it do? (*She
            isn't too keen.*) We'll all join in, we'll do it as well.
            Dan, you'll be in it, won't you?

DAN   Are you kidding? I'm the most superstitious man who
            ever lived. You're looking at the man who poured a
            pint of beer over his head before every home game
            for nearly a whole season.

BIRGITTA   Why?

DAN   Tried it once, and Stoke won.

            (IAN *and* BIRGITTA *look at each other and shrug.*)

BILL   Come on Monica. (*He goes over to the wall chart,
            which has a map of Italy on it.*) Look, Turin is up
            here, and Majorca is down here. The bay faces
            south, so we're facing . . . east, so Italy's up that way.
            (*Points diagonally off stage left.*)

IAN   Well count me out.

BILL   Surprise surprise. Monica?

MONICA   (*gives in*) All right. You've all got to concentrate . . .
            (*Deep breaths.*) Ready? (*She starts to giggle.*) I can't
            believe you want to do this . . .

DAN   Yeah, come on.

MONICA   Ok. Imagine . . . going over to the door, along the
            corridor . . . we're going down in the lift, out into the
            lobby, past the reception, past that bloke with the
            glass eye who keeps trying to touch my bottom . . .

BILL   Hurry it up for God's sake. There's only twelve
            minutes left.

MONICA   You've got to concentrate . . .

BILL   Yes yes yes . . .

MONICA	Ok, out onto the main road, we're going down to the beach, down to the sea, and Italy's right over there, over the horizon, and out we go over the sea . . . (DAN, *now really into it, spreads his arms out as if flying, and* IAN *can't resist taking the piss.*)
IAN	What do you think you're doing?
DAN	Steering. Shut up.
MONICA	Right, the sea's rushing away beneath us . . . and there, straight ahead, it's the coast, it's Italy . . .
IAN	Oh my God!
BILL DAN	} What?!
IAN	Passports! You forgot your passports!
BIRGITTA	Shut up, Ian.
MONICA	We're on the outskirts of Turin, looking for the stadium, we can see the floodlights down in front of us, can you see?
BILL	Yes.
DAN	Um . . . yeah . . .
BILL	Carry on.
MONICA	We go down, we can see the crowd, the pitch, the players. I can see Gary in his number ten shirt.
BILL	Make him score.
MONICA	How? How can I?
BILL	Make it happen.
DAN	Come on England . . .
BILL	Come on . . .
MONICA	Come on Gary, do it for me . . .

(*They are intense, willing a goal, but they don't really know what to do next.* IAN *and* BIRGITTA *watch the television with mounting disbelief.*)

IAN   Hey, you want to watch this . . .

(*Crowd noise erupts from the television, as Gary Lineker scores for England.*)

Good God!

(BIRGITTA *swears in German.* DAN *looks at the screen in disbelief, then goes crazy, running around the room. He and* BILL *hug each other and jump up and down.*)

DAN   (*to* MONICA) You little beauty!

(DAN *grabs* MONICA *and kisses her, then he decides to kiss* BIRGITTA *as well.* IAN *waits his turn to snog* BIRGITTA, *but finds he is waiting rather longer then he would like.* BILL'S *celebrations include his "Roger Milla" dance.*)

BILL   That can't have been a coincidence, can it?

MONICA   Of course it can.

BILL   The last thing you said was "Come on Gary, do it for me . . . " and then Gary did it for you.

MONICA   So?

BILL   Well so do it again.

MONICA   No.

BILL   Monica, come on . . .

MONICA   I can't make things happen, Bill, I was just humouring you. It's a coincidence, that's all.

(MONICA *goes outside to the balcony.* BILL *is torn between the game and following her. The game wins.* DAN *and* BIRGITTA *finish their snog,* IAN *puckers up, eyes shut, but* BIRGITTA *sits down.*)

DAN   One-one. What about that, eh? We can still do this you know. I wish I'd known about this flying thing before. I'd have had Stoke back in the first ages ago.

BIRGITTA   It was incredible.

DAN   What's she doing now? Is she doing another goal?

BILL   Just a coincidence she said.

IAN   (*hums the "Twilight Zone" theme, then continues in cod American accent*) Ding ding ding ding . . . Coincidence? The human mind is a vast uncharted land, and which of us knows what secrets lie beyond the boundaries of . . . its Twilight Zone? Ding ding ding ding . . .

DAN   Come on then, lads, you're on your own.

BIRGITTA   What is this "ding ding ding ding"? Is it meant to be a train?

IAN   Um . . . oh, listen Dan, did you hear that?

DAN   What?

IAN   Monica calling you, out on the balcony. I expect she probably wants to talk to you about something really important.

DAN   What's wrong with you? Can't you see there's football on?

           (IAN, *thwarted, shuts up. We go out to the balcony.*)

MONICA   (*on the balcony*) Now listen to me, Gary Lineker. What do you think you're up to? I can't have you going real on me. It's been a game of two halves, Gary, ninety minutes on the day, and so on, but now it's time to get on the coach with the others and wave goodbye, go on. Fuck off back to Michelle, go on.

           Bill. I'm sorry, Bill. I'm leaving you. I never meant to hurt you, but I'm certain it's best for both of us. I'm leaving you after eight years of sometimes not too unhappy marriage, and I'm going to live with Dan Hudson.

DAN   (*inside, reacting to something on the telly*) Ooooyah! You bastard!

MONICA   Oh God, I'm not am I? Dan. Dan, I'm sorry, I'm leaving you. I never meant to hurt you but I'm certain it's best for both of us. I'm leaving you after eight months of sneaking around and occasional weekends in Europe, and I'm going back to my husband.

         (*Then the full-time whistle.* BILL *exhales loudly.* DAN *and* BIRGITTA *share a look.*)

BILL   Extra time. (*He sits back in his chair.*)

IAN   Oh God, you don't mean there's more?

         (BILL *exits to the balcony to see* MONICA *and get some air.* DAN *and* BIRGITTA *are obviously excluding* IAN, *and to get attention he starts talking about* BILL'S *World Cup wall chart. During this speech,* DAN *and* BIRGITTA *leave, more or less surreptitiously.*)

IAN   Look. Bill's World Cup wall chart. You know Monica burnt his first one. Between you, me and the door post, I don't think things are going too well for those two. Work's going badly for him. I know that. I don't think he's up to it, frankly. He takes refuge in this sort of thing. Look at the care he's put into it. Four different coloured pens. It's sad, really. It's like he retreats into his own little world because people don't listen to him any more . . .

         (*He looks round.* DAN *and* BIRGITTA - *his audience - have left the room.*)

         Hello . . . ? Birgitta . . . ?

         (*He searches for her, checking other rooms. Back on the balcony . . .*)

BILL   It's odd.

MONICA   Bill.

BILL   You're amazing.

MONICA	I've got to tell you something.
	(IAN *joins them on the balcony*.)
IAN	Where's Dan? And Birgitta?
MONICA	I don't know.
BILL	I reckon they're getting a sweat up in a broom cupboard somewhere.
MONICA	Would Dan do that?
IAN	I'm sure Birgitta wouldn't, would she?
BILL	Oh, she would, she would.
IAN	She would not.
BILL	She would.
IAN	How do you know?
MONICA	Yes, how do you know?
BILL	Erm . . . she and I have a sort of bet.
MONICA	A bet?
BILL	The deal was: if England win, she has to have sex with an Englishman.
MONICA	She didn't say she would, did she?
BILL	Oh, but she did.
MONICA	What about if Germany win? What do you have to do? Have sex with a German girl, perhaps?
BILL	Don't be daft.
IAN	Am I the Englishman?
BILL	Not any more, I don't think.
	(IAN *goes back into the room*.)
MONICA	So Dan's muscled in on your bet. Don't you resent that?

BILL   Naaah, good for him. You can't begrudge him, can
            you. He's such a good bloke.

MONICA   Listen to me Bill . . .

            (BILL *goes back into the room.* MONICA *follows.*)

BILL   Oh no, not now, Monica. Whatever you want to say
            can wait till the end of the game. We're thirty minutes
            from the World Cup final, for Christ's sake.

IAN   Unless there's penalties.

BILL   Forty five minutes.

MONICA   Yes, and then we're in the final and we'll have to wait
            until the end of the final. And then we'll have to wait
            till the end of the penalties, and then have to wait till
            Gary Lineker goes up and gets the trophy, then till
            the team bus drives back through Luton, then it'll be
            next season, and the most important game for Spurs
            since the last most important important game for
            Spurs, and then we'll have to wait a bit more because
            we're just so used to waiting that nothing else is
            possible.

BILL   Look. (*Pause.*) It won't be Gary Lineker getting the
            trophy. Terry Butcher's the captain.

            (MONICA *is frustrated and angry. She leaves the
            room.* BILL *and* IAN *are left.* BILL *doesn't know what
            to say.*)

BILL   They must be tired, eh?

IAN   How long before they start again?

BILL   Not long. Couple of minutes.

IAN   Dan will want to be back for that, won't he?

BILL   Aren't you pissed off? I thought you were "on a
            promise".

IAN   It wouldn't be good publicity for Dan, would it . . . ?

BILL   What?

IAN	What was this bet again? If England win . . . ? They haven't won yet, have they?
BILL	It was just meant to be a joke.
IAN	A joke? It's not a joke. Putting a jar of pickled onions in somebody's case with the top loosened, *that's* a joke.
BILL	You're a sad fucker, aren't you?
IAN	Oooh, hallo Mr Pot my name's Mr Kettle.
	(*They have nothing more to say. Suddenly* DAN *re-enters carrying the furry elephant. Chucks it off the balcony.*)
DAN	Has it started yet?
BILL	Just.
IAN	Where's Birgitta?
DAN	Oh, we went for a stroll, she met Graeme Souness in the toilet - can't quite work that one out - and she went to the bar with him. Do you think Wright's got it in him?
IAN	It? I thought if you had "it" you had to hand it to Shilton.
DAN	Good, Ian, that was almost funny.
BILL	Did you just do it with Birgitta?
DAN	(*makes a non-committal grunting noise*) Where's Monica?
BILL	Having a lusty lesbian romp with Birgitta while Graeme Souness watches.
DAN	Let's hope so.
IAN	Did you do it with Birgitta?
DAN	Ah, the lovely Birgitta . . .
IAN	Watch it, that's my fiancée you're talking about.

DAN   Does she know that?

IAN   Did you do it with her?

DAN   Was there time?

IAN   Of course there was. You were gone nearly five whole minutes.

DAN   Perhaps I boiled an egg as well. (*Turning to telly and* BILL.) Have they brought any subs on?

BILL   Steven.

IAN   (*snaps*) You're just an animal, aren't you, you ride roughshod over everything. Some of the things you get up to in your books, I couldn't believe it. From brothels in Bogota, venereal diseases in Venezuela, Dan Hudson kicks shit in everybody's faces.

DAN   You liked them enough to make me an offer.

BILL   Ian? Ian made you an offer? When?

DAN   Couple of months ago.

BILL   A couple of *months* ago? (*Unable to comprehend.*) What sort of offer?

DAN   He said he could get a better deal for me at Hutchinson's.

BILL   How? He doesn't work for Hutchinson's. He doesn't work for anybody since that business at Tate's.

DAN   Hutchinson's would have taken him on though, if . . .

BILL   . . . if he'd brought them you, you mean. You little shit . . .

DAN   I couldn't have gone with them, though.

BILL   Don't tell me you thought it was unethical.

DAN   No. There was a Hutchinson used to play for Chelsea. He scored twice against us in 1970-71.

(BILL *turns on* IAN *and backs him towards the balcony.* DAN *squats in front of the television, leaving them to it.*)

BILL   Ian, when this game ends I'm going to throw you off the balcony.

IAN   You too? Look it's just business, Bill.

BILL   Hence all the questions about how so-and-so's getting along, and what Tate's planning for next year. God almighty . . . and you know that if I lose Dan I'll be out on my arse, don't you? When I think how long we've been friends. Friends!

(BILL *suddenly runs out of steam and goes vacant. He seems miles away.* IAN *stares at* BILL, *waiting for more wrath, but none comes.* DAN *is watching the telly.*)

DAN   Ooooh! Look at that! He's a fucking maniac! Gazza, diving in like that.

(BILL *snaps back to life, and hurries over to see.*)

BILL   It's going to be a yellow card.

DAN   Oh he can't book him for that!

BILL   He can . . . he's going to miss the final. Yes, there it goes.

DAN   Oh, no . . .

BILL   He's going to miss the final.

IAN   He's crying, look.

DAN   Oh yes, but imagine missing the World Cup final.

(IAN *shrugs.*)

Come on Gazza, pull yourself together, this one's not over yet.

(BIRGITTA *enters and smartly turns the television off.*)

BILL   What are you doing, for Christ's sake?

DAN	Birgitta!
BILL	(*trying to reach past her*) Now look, Birgitta. If you don't turn it on . . .
BIRGITTA	What? Will you hit me?
BILL	What?
BIRGITTA	Monica is unhappy.
DAN	I'm unhappy. You've turned the World Cup off.

(MONICA *enters.*)

BILL	Monica . . . (*Indicates TV.*)
BIRGITTA	I'm going for a walk, Ian.
IAN	Perhaps Graeme Souness would like to go with you.
BIRGITTA	(*grabbing him by the wrist*) Ian, I'm going for a walk.
IAN	All right, I'm coming.

(BIRGITTA *and* IAN *leave.*)

MONICA	Bill. There's something I have to tell you.
BILL	I know. Turn the telly on.
MONICA	I've been seeing Dan.

(DAN *groans and covers his eyes.*)

BILL	I know. Turn the telly on.
MONICA	Dan?
DAN	Monica.
MONICA	Aren't you going to say something?
DAN	Turn the telly on.
MONICA	No. No no no. You're going to decide this for yourselves. You're not going to let twenty two complete strangers two thousand miles away determine whether you're happy or miserable. It's my turn. You talk about this, it's your lives, your real

lives, and whatever you decide we're going to do will be all right by me. I'm surrendering myself this time. I don't want to watch the match, just tell me the result.

(MONICA *goes out onto the balcony.* DAN *and* BILL *avoid eye contact awkwardly for a moment or two, then both start talking at the same instant.*)

BILL   You first.

DAN   No, you.

MONICA   (*on the balcony, to herself*) It's just tossing a coin, that's what it is. My mother used to say: "If you really can't tell what you want to do, just toss a coin." Then if you find yourself saying "Ok, best of three" - then you know what it is you really want.

(*Back inside the room.*)

BILL   I was just going to say, a thing that Monica always says.

DAN   What?

BILL   She always says that men, when men get together, they never talk about the things that they care about, about their emotions, they just talk about football.

DAN   That's crap, isn't it?

BILL   Yeah, it's crap.

(*Pause.*)

DAN   That was a goal, Lineker's goal, wasn't it?

BILL   Yeah, just swept it past two of them and tucked it in. Great goal. Our goal. It'll be in the title sequence of Grandstand into the 21st century, that goal.

(DAN *does a cursory bit of acting out the goal.*)

DAN   It will, it will . . . See, he went past them, then he put it behind them. It was a striker's goal . . .

(*Another pause.*)

BILL   You see, what she doesn't realise, Monica, is that the things that men care about, that really matter, that they really get emotional about . . . they *are* football.

DAN   Exactly. We've got to think what's really important here . . .

BILL   It's extra time in the World Cup semi-final. I can't believe she turned it off, I mean, what are we, kids?

DAN   No, we're grown men, we can sort this out between us. No need to get hysterical.

BILL   Absolutely not.

DAN   Let's just face the facts, deal with the practicalities . . .

BILL   It's England in the semi-final of the World Cup. I can't believe she switched that off.

DAN   And Spanish commentary as well. How are we going to know if they scored while we weren't watching?

BILL   Exactly! Exactly!

DAN   We could just switch it on again . . . ?

BILL   She'd hear.

DAN   Sound right off?

BILL   No, she'd hear, she'd hear.

DAN   She's outside.

BILL   All right, switch it on then.

MONICA'S
VOICE   (*from the balcony*) Don't you dare!

BILL   See?

DAN   God! I can't stand this. Look. I've been sleeping with Monica, and I'm sorry. I'll jump off the balcony if you want. I will. Just say the word.

(BILL *shakes his head.*)

DAN   Did you know before?

BILL   I wondered. Something you said earlier on, when
               Germany scored.

DAN   Huh? Anyway I know this is embarrassing, but you
               decide what you want to do, between the two of you.
               I think I ought to find another publisher, just to save,
               you know, it's embarrassing for you . . .

BILL   Well there's no need . . .

DAN   Not Ian. You know I wouldn't do that, don't you?
               You know me, don't you?

               (BILL *shrugs. Pause.*)

DAN   What's going to happen?

BILL   Don't know.

DAN   Telly on and find out?

BILL   (*momentarily distracted, but then*) . . . yeah.

               (*They switch the television on.* MONICA *screams in
               frustration. After a moment or two she comes in and
               watches them.*)

DAN   What's going on, they're all sitting down . . . ?

BILL   Oh Jesus, oh fuck. It's penalties.

DAN   I can't watch penalties, I can't. I never watch them.

MONICA   Well?

BILL   Penalties.

               (IAN *comes back in with the furry elephant.*)

IAN   What was that scream? Shall I call the police?

               (DAN *takes the furry elephant and boots it back over
               the balcony.*)

What's going on? I thought you'd be at each other's throats by now.

BILL   It's penalties.

MONICA   Something else I wanted to tell you, Bill. Earlier on, Ian tried to blackmail me into helping him poach Dan from you.

IAN   As a joke.

BILL   If England lose this . . . if England lose this, Ian, my one happiness will be that after tomorrow I will never see you again.

MONICA   Hoorah!

IAN   Cuckold! Oooh, if only Birgitta could hear me say that.

BILL   Dan, I bet you that if England lose you daren't throw Ian off the balcony.

DAN   Don't, Bill.

BILL   I dare you.

IAN   Ha ha ha ha, now then Dan. Spanish prisons are terrible. You saw "Midnight Express" . . . ?

BILL   I quadruple dare you.

DAN   I can't watch. I never watch penalties.

MONICA   Never?

DAN   Never. I took a penalty once, in a match. As I ran up I thought: "I can't watch this". Shut my eyes.

IAN   And you scored, right?

DAN   Hit the corner flag.

BILL   Oh God, I can't watch it either . . . I can't bear it.

IAN   (*attempting to curry favour, conciliatory*) Do you want me to tell you what happens? Yes?

(They don't reply. IAN *scurries round in front of the set and begins to describe for them.)*

IAN   Looks like it's going to be England first.

BILL   That's good. The pitch'll probably deteriorate by the fifth penalty.

IAN   Here's the first one. It's Gary Lineker. He's running up now . . . straight down the middle. One-nil.

BILL   Gary Lineker, the Queen Mother of football.

MONICA   Is it possible, sweet lady, for your laugh to be as beautiful as your eyes?

IAN   This one's called Brehme. Two goals in Italia 90, apparently . . . Thumps it in. One-one.

DAN   Fucking bollocks to it. What a shagwanking disaster.

BILL   When I think how long we've been friends. Friends!

IAN   Next it's Beardsley . . . Top right hand corner. Two-one.

DAN   Yes!

BILL   Go on you bastard, get in there!

MONICA   You're exactly the same, you two.

IAN   Who's this . . . ? *(Peering at the screen.)* Matthaus. *(He pronounces it "Matt-house".)* . . . Shilton goes the right way, but nowhere near it. Two-two.

DAN   Shilton. He's like a wildebeest with a drink problem.

BILL   I know. I know.

DAN   I'll find another publisher to save . . . you know, it's embarrassing for you . . .

BILL   You know if I lose Dan Hudson I'll be out on my arse, don't you?

IAN   All right, for England this is Platt. Here he comes . . . keeper's got a hand to it . . .

DAN BILL	} No!

IAN   . . . but it's gone in. Three-two.

MONICA   May the best team win.

BILL   Certainly not. May England win.

MONICA   What about if Germany win?

DAN   We've played some terrific games together. Really
            entertaining fixtures . . .

IAN   Next German is Riedle . . . whacks it in. Shilton no
            chance. Three-three.

MONICA   Take me away from all this.

DAN   Prime minister: Jimmy Greenhoff.

BILL   The most important important game for twenty four
            years . . . I can't bear it . . .

IAN   Who's this one? Pearce. He looks really nervous . . .

            (DAN *covers his ears*, BILL *puts his hands to his
            mouth*, MONICA *shuts her eyes. They shut out "evil".
            The staging should maybe echo the "willing the goal"
            bit from earlier.*)

IAN   And Pearce . . .

DAN   Scores! Four-three to England!

            (DAN, BILL *and* MONICA *react.*)

            But it's not time to celebrate yet. The England
            players sit exhausted in a huddle in the centre circle.
            And this is Olaf Thon, the number twenty . . . and
            Shilton has saved it! Thon blasted it towards the top
            right-hand corner, and Shilton flung himself full
            length and headed the ball away!

MONICA   So now England are only one kick away from the
            World Cup final. Lineker steps up to take it. He's
            taken one already, but under the new rules he is
            allowed to take up to three.

DAN   And he scores! England are in the World Cup final!

BILL   Lineker disappears under a mountain of white shirts, the players are ecstatic. Bobby Robson - Sir Bobby now, of course - is weeping with joy!

DAN   So is Butcher.

MONICA   And Beardsley.

DAN   And of course Gazza, poor Gazza, barred from the final. But what's this? A small man in a red cloak is running onto the pitch . . . it's the Pope! He's giving Gazza confession.

BILL   Gazza is apologising for the foul, and I can just hear the Pope and he's saying that if Gazza does two Hail Marys he can play in the final.

MONICA   Lineker's hugging Gazza and weeping to the bottom of his soul. It's the greatest moment of a great day.

DAN   And I think Trevor's down on the pitch with Gary . . . Trevor?

               (*Sound effects of crowd noise, and we hear a taped interview with Lineker.*)

TREVOR   Gary Lineker . . . you've scored the winning goal to
BROOKING   get us to the World Cup final. How do you feel?

GARY   Trevor, that is such a stupid question. Obviously I'm
LINEKER   absolutely gutted.

               (DAN, MONICA and BILL *laugh.*)

TREVOR   Fantastic when the Pope ran onto the pitch?
BROOKING

GARY   Oh yes. I thought it was Father Christmas at first, it's
LINEKER   been such an incredible day.

TREVOR   Now what about the final?
BROOKING

GARY LINEKER	Trevor, I'm sorry, I've got to go and see some friends, they need me.
TREVOR BROOKING	Thanks Gary . . . Back to the studio. 'Triffic.

(Taped interview ends.)

MONICA	That's us, he's coming to see us.
BILL	Is he?
DAN	Yeah!
MONICA	Yes he is.
	Gary's coming!
IAN	What is happening? The Germans have won. Aren't you interested?
BILL	His legs are brown, his name is Gary, He's the man Monica's going to marry.
IAN	Dan. We should talk again about Hutchinson's, you know. I mean, I know you don't like me, but you don't really know me, and at least I'm not raving bonkers. I mean look at him.

("Nessun Dorma" begins to fill the air. BILL is beaming seraphically.)

DAN	Gary's going to take us to Rome for the final.
IAN	You what? Gary who? Gary Lineker? You don't think Gary Lineker's going to turn up here, do you?

(The music swells, crowd cheering added in. Lights change and GARY LINEKER comes in. It is a messianic entrance. He falls to his knees as though he has scored a great goal, and DAN, MONICA and BILL mob him, and dance round him as though he is a maypole. All this in slow motion.)

BILL	Monica and I are finished, but it doesn't matter now you're here, Gary.

DAN   Monica doesn't want me either, not now you're here,
             Gary.

MONICA   Dan meant nothing to me, Gary. I'm sorry I shouted
             at you. Do your farts really smell of perfume?

             (GARY *drops one, and nods.*)

DAN   Can you take us to the final, Gary?

             (GARY *gives* DAN *three tickets.*)

BILL   Can I have a cigarette, Gary?

             (GARY *gives* BILL *a fag, lights one himself.*)

             Fags don't give you cancer any more, do they, Gary?

             (GARY *shakes his head.*)

DAN   Stoke are going to get promotion now, aren't they,
             Gary?

             (GARY *nods.*)

BILL   I'd love to publish "My World Cup Glory" by Gary
             Lineker, Gary.

             (GARY *hands him a manuscript.*)

             Excellent!

MONICA   Kiss me Gary.

BILL
DAN   } Kiss her, Gary!

             (GARY *kisses* MONICA. BILL *and* DAN *cheer.* GARY
             *steps back magnificently, and brandishes a red card
             at* IAN. BILL, DAN *and* MONICA *cheer.*)

MONICA   And so . . . to Rome!

             (GARY *does a cartwheel. Music reaches massive
             crescendo.* BILL, MONICA, *and* DAN *cheer and cling
             onto him. He leads them off, in a slow motion goal
             celebrating mode.* IAN'S *look of bafflement is more
             than any actor has ever achieved hitherto. Lights*

return to normal as "Nessun Dorma" ends abruptly.
IAN *is utterly confused, and may well not be the only
one. He has not seen Lineker. In the preceding
section there has been noise, action and confusion.
Now there is quiet. He sits with a bottle of beer in his
hand.* BIRGITTA *returns.*)

BIRGITTA　　Hallo . . . where are the others?

IAN　　I don't know. Gone. The game ended, and they sort
of . . . went potty. What they saw, and what I saw . . .
maybe I'm potty.

BIRGITTA　　You Robinsons. You are all potty. So who won?

IAN　　Didn't you see the penalties?

BIRGITTA　　No, I was talking with Graeme Souness in the bar.

IAN　　Surely he was watching it?

BIRGITTA　　Ah, no, he is Scottish. He is too hard, he was telling
me. He was very helpful, he told me all about
Scotland, which is where I'm going for my
honeymoon.

IAN　　Honeymoon? Your honeymoon?

BIRGITTA　　Yes.

IAN　　You're getting married?

BIRGITTA　　This is my last summer as a single girl.

IAN　　Oh. But you made a bet with Bill, didn't you?

BIRGITTA　　Ha ha ha, yes I did, I bet that if England won the
game, I would sleep with an Englishman.

IAN　　So . . . have you?

BIRGITTA　　How can I have? The game has only just ended.

(*A knock at the door.* IAN *goes to answer it.*)

I don't even know who won.

IAN   (*off*) Oh yes. Thank you, senor . . . No change, sorry.

             (IAN *comes back in with champagne.*)

             Somebody ordered some champagne.

BIRGITTA   So, Ian . . .? Who won?

IAN   Um . . . England won.

             (*He pops open the champagne and pours her a glass.*)

             England won on penalties.

             (IAN *swigs champagne from the bottle. Blackout.*)

TRENCH KISS

Arthur Smith

TRENCH KISS was first presented by Rupert Gavin for
Incidental Theatre at the Pleasance Theatre, Edinburgh in
August 1991 as part of the Edinburgh Fringe Festival, with the
following cast:

JIM	Arthur Smith
SALLY	Caroline Quentin
JASPER	Ben Miller

Directed by Audrey Cook
Designed by Bethia Jane Green
Music arranged by Mark Bradley

Scene One

A military graveyard in Ypres. As the house lights go down, the Last Post is heard. SALLY *and* JIM *enter and look gravely at some gravestones.*

JIM   (*reading gravestones*) Soldier of the Great War known unto God. Maybe that's him . . . Thomas Bowlby, died aged 24, May 7th, 1917: Peace at last after life's troubled dream . . . Soldier of the Great War, known unto God . . . Maybe that's him . . . Maurice Atkinson, died aged 21 November 3rd, 1914. Never shall their memory be blotted out.

SALLY   Sally Hunt, died of boredom, 14th July, 1988. Never shall her tedium be surpassed.

JIM   (*reading another*) Soldier of the Great War known unto God.

SALLY   Maybe that's him.

JIM   (*ignoring her*) Captain Geoffrey Keating, died October 29th, 1918. God, so close to the end.

SALLY   Are you going to read all of these gravestones out?

JIM   Yes.

SALLY   Jim, there are twelve thousand of them.

JIM   Do you have any understanding of why I'm doing this?

SALLY   'To commune with your grandad.'

JIM   There's another reason. A more important reason.

SALLY   What?

JIM   To annoy you. That's what you seem to imagine anyway.

SALLY   Well for Christ's sake it is boring. This place is
             like a three-dimensional telephone directory.

JIM   Telephone directories already are three-
             dimensional.

SALLY   Pendant.

JIM   Private Lindsay Cameron. Scottish Highland
             Regiment. Died December 31st, 1916.

SALLY   Bit of a shit Hogmanay for him then.

             (JIM *looks angry, but then laughs.*)

JIM   Is it really boring for you?

SALLY   I don't know, it's warm, it's quite pretty round
             here, I quite like looking round graveyards
             sometimes, but this one, all these ones round
             here, they're so homogenised.

JIM   Homogenised? What, like milk?

SALLY   In a way. I prefer my cemeteries unpasteurised.
             My idea of a good cemetery is the graves all
             higgledy-piggledy, overgrown, or leaning. In a
             decent graveyard you should be able to have a
             surreptitious fuck in the corner of it.

JIM   I should write to the Commonwealth War graves
             Commission about that.

SALLY   This place is so regulated, it's just row after neat
             row of well-tended, identically sized, identically
             coloured gravestones. I mean if McDonalds ever
             went into designing cemeteries this is what
             they'd come up with.

JIM   Well, normally lots and lots of people don't all
             die in the same place at the same time. That's
             war.

SALLY   That's what I don't like. It's all about war. If you
             half close your eyes, you can see men coming

towards you, wave after wave, all looking the same, all standing erect, at attention.

JIM   (*tries this*) No I don't see it. It would have to be the Royal Pigmy Regiment.

SALLY   Let's go back to the hotel.

JIM   One more.

(SALLY *groans.*)

JIM   It's only a little one, only about a hundred and fifty tombstones. We can do it in ten minutes.

SALLY   Let's go back to the hotel, have a bath, have a beer, have a meal, dancing, let's go dancing.

JIM   There's nowhere to dance in Ypres. We're in Belgium for God's sake.

SALLY   This must be the only place in the world with a hundred and sixty cemeteries and no disco.

JIM   Come on, you've been to Basildon.

SALLY   A beer. Surely a beer. Don't you fancy a beer?

JIM   One more.

SALLY   Fisties.

JIM   All right.

(*They play fisties. She loses.*)

SALLY   Bollocks.

JIM   Come on then.

(*They exit. Music.*)

Scene Two

The lights rise on JASPER, *wearing civilian clothes, circa 1915.*

JASPER   I've joined up! Good God I've joined up. What a
                relief.

                (*He pulls a white feather from his pocket.*)

                I got two of these in one morning. Rather
                pleasant soft little thing.

                Two young ladies. Two white feathers. After
                college I adjourned to a public house with Jack.
                Jack is an extraordinary and entertaining fellow.
                Not only does he claim to be an anarchist, a
                communist and a pacifist, he is also able to belch
                the names of all the countries of the world.
                Furthermore, he has taught me this trick.
                (*Belches.*) India, Rhodesia. But you have to
                disregard his claptrap. He relishes his white
                feathers, he has created a display of them in his
                bedroom. Under each white feather is a card
                with a description of the lady who presented it to
                him. One of them just said, "Prim, grim and a fat
                behind". He has been beaten twice lately.
                People tell me I should not associate with him
                now, but he does make me laugh. Prim, Grim and
                a fat behind. (*Belches.*) Belgium.

                (*The lights fade.*)

Scene Three

In the next cemetery, SALLY *and* JIM *are looking at gravestones.*

SALLY   Lots of July Firsts, 1916.

JIM   That was the first day of the Battle of the
                Somme. There were twenty thousand British
                soldiers killed that day.

SALLY   Twenty thousand . . . that's a lot.

JIM   Yes.

SALLY   Less than Arsenal's home gate mind.

JIM   But a lot bigger than Hibs'. Most of them were
               killed in the first hour. They attacked at 7.30 and
               they were just mown down.

SALLY   Seven thirty, eight thirty. That's when I get up.
               Twenty thousand in an hour. That is a lot. That's
               like ten thousand in half an hour.

JIM   Five thousand in fifteen minutes.

SALLY   About one thousand every three minutes.

JIM   Three hundred a minute.

SALLY   Five every second.

JIM   Da da da da da. Five. (*He clicks his fingers.*)
               Killed.

SALLY   What a joyous holiday this is. Other couples go
               on holiday to Italy or India, what do I get? Ten
               days in Southern Belgium.

JIM   We played fisties, you lost.

               (*Blackout.*)

                        Scene Four

The lights rise on JASPER.

JASPER   I am an ignorant, headstrong boy who will get
               killed for no good reason. That's what father
               says. He must be the only solicitor in London
               who agrees with Ramsey MacDonald.

               I think what chiefly irritated him was that I have
               to pay a three pounds entrance fee. And then . . .
               (*He winces at the memory.*) . . . I asked him to
               loan me the money. That's when he blew his top.
               If I'm going to get killed he shouldn't have to
               pay for it. What, he says, what if you come back
               with no legs, and I said I'll just have to take the
               motorbus more often. He didn't laugh. Poor
               Father, he still misses Mother. (*Pause - so does*
               JASPER.) I did a year in the O.T.C.

(*He does a mime of bayonetting a German on the ground. Hard to get bayonet out. He puts his left foot on the German and pulls it out.*)

I was certainly very good at bayonetting sacks of hay. If the Germans decide to recruit sacks of hay instead of men I shall be the scourge of all France.

(*Pause.*)

One of the most important elements in the art of manipulating a bayonet, we were told, is "the killing face". You must, as you bear down on your victim, adopt an expression of frenzied violence. I practised my killing face on my classmates. They were unimpressed. (*He does it.*) Who wouldn't be? The sacks of hay remained impassive.

Oh, it will probably all be over by the time I get there. It can't last much longer. It's already been going a year, a whole year. I shan't be killed, other people get killed. Sidney Richardson, Herbert Rowland, they were in my class at the City. Other people get killed. People whose surnames start with 'R'. They get killed.

(*Blackout.*)

Scene Five

JIM *and* SALLY *sat at a table in a cafe in Ypres with two cocktails at which* JIM *is looking ruefully. Music plays, "Ca Plane Pour Moi", Plastique Bertrand.*)

JIM   Deux bières, surely that was comprehensible.

SALLY   Face it, Jim, they can't understand your French. You speak French like the queen and anyway they're Flemish.

JIM   Then they should blow their noses.

SALLY   (*laughs*) That's a rubbish joke.

JIM   Yeah.

SALLY   It's quite pretty isn't it, Ypres?

JIM   Yeah.

SALLY   Feels quite old.

JIM   Yeah. It isn't of course.

SALLY   Isn't it?

JIM   No. It was smashed up during the War and they rebuilt it exactly as it was.

SALLY   Did they? Why?

JIM   I suppose they wanted it to feel the same as it was before the War. After all that they didn't fancy anything too new.

SALLY   You can see their point. How much have we had to drink?

JIM   A carafe of wine. Each. A pastis each. And deux (*Glaring at his cocktail.*) 'bières'.

SALLY   We ought to eat.

JIM   Yeah. I can't be bothered.

SALLY   No.

JIM   Shall I read you a poem?

SALLY   No.

JIM   Soldiers probably sat in this cafe, got pissed, then got killed before they'd got rid of their hangover.

SALLY   Good cure for it.

JIM   I'd like to be pissed when I die.

SALLY   You probably will be.

JIM Lots of these soldiers were, they used to give them half a pint of scotch before they went over the top.

SALLY Yes, well you're not going to stand up to be shot at if you're sober are you? Once you've had a couple of drinks though, "Yeah, come on I'm over here Fritz, see if you can get one between my eyes".

JIM Some of them got so pissed they passed out before they could get out of the trench.

SALLY Thereby saving their lives.

JIM Temporarily.

(*Pause.*)

SALLY Why do you like all this stuff?

JIM It's history. It's the start of our age. Everything that's happened since happened because of this. Everything.

SALLY Everything?

JIM Everything.

SALLY What about ABBA?

JIM In a way, yes. In some sense the battle of the Somme made ABBA possible.

SALLY Please God ask him not to explain that to me.

JIM Didn't they do 'Waterloo'?

SALLY That's all very grand, but I don't see what it has to do with us traipsing round cemeteries, ticking off names of dead soldiers.

JIM Why do you think I'm interested in it?

SALLY Because you're a boy. Boys fight 'em and boys like 'em. Whatever you say your reasons are, somewhere in it all is you dressed in uniform doing something exciting in the mud. Doing male bonding and bayonetting Germans. Writing poems and shagging French tarts.

JIM   Hmph.

SALLY   You're not here with me now are you? You're here seventy years ago with all your pals with funny names, Herbert and Reginald and Alfred and Syd. You and your love affair with this war. This isn't a holiday. It's you having a mind wank.

JIM   Do you have to swear so much?

SALLY   Yes I think I do. Do you think wars are good?

JIM   Well, they get you out of the house.

(*Lights change. Music.*)

Scene Six

JASPER, *now in World War I uniform, and looking in a mirror.*

JASPER   This is a splendid opportunity to impress the ladies. I am marvellously handsome. For God, King and Country, but also for Enoch Bennett's sister, Emily.

               Of course what would really set it off nicely would be a little wound stripe. Well a normal size stripe, but a little wound. A decent little wound. Visible but not unsightly. Elegant and painless.

               (*He brushes his hand through his hair and then as though someone has made a comment about it, looks at his hand.*)

               Oh yes, I was in action at Le Cateau, more cake, Emily. Le Cateau, Neuve Chapelle. Etaples, Bapaume, such romantic words. Cambrai, Bapaume. Let me be sent to France, not Turkey. I wonder when I shall be sent to the Front. "The

Front" . . . "I'm going to the Front." What I
secretly hope for is a brief period at the Front
and a long period at the back.

Germans are going to try and kill me and the
police are not going to arrest them.

(*He has put his jacket on. The sleeves are too
long.*)

Oh no, the sleeves. Look at the sleeves! I look
like Maxie London.

(*Lights change. Music.*)

Scene Seven

Still in the cafe.

JIM   Dick Firham, that was it, Dick Firham. He was the
             last person I hit. We were both nine. I used to
             beat him up every Thursday to establish that I
             was the best fighter in our class, which, as you
             can imagine, was quite an important and
             respected position. The trouble was the boys in
             our class were all rather weedy compared to the
             boys in Miss. Gomm's class. They were brutes.
             They virtually had beards. I played football with
             them Thursday evenings and they'd ask "who is
             the best fighter in your class?," and I'd always
             say "Dick Firham". So they used to beat him up
             on Fridays.

SALLY   I bet the weekends were a relief to him.

JIM   Dick Firham, he was an idiot.

SALLY   That's not an answer.

JIM   That's what I'm saying. I'm not violent. I abhor
             violence, it's disgusting; but my Dad was in a
             war, my grandad was, I don't know, I feel I'm
             missing out.

SALLY   I thought you said war is ninety-nine percent tedium and one percent frenetic action . . . (*Laughs.*) . . . like our sex life.

JIM   Except without the frenetic action (*Laughs.*) People who've survived it say that everything after becomes mundane. There's war and everything else is trivial pursuit and I think fuck it, that's not fair, 'cos I've taken all the drugs, I've been pissed beyond the ken of human kind, I've had sex up a mountain, I've masturbated over Gloria Hunniford, I mean I've been naughty but . . . but throwing bread rolls in a restaurant will never be as exciting as the possibility of having your head blown off. My body has never made that amount of adrenalin. I wonder what it's like to be 'in extremis.'

SALLY   I give up on you. If you want danger why don't you go and do hang gliding off a cliff, or play Russian Roulette, or go down to a disco and call the bouncer a cunt?

JIM   Because I don't have to. I wouldn't choose it, you'd be mad to.

SALLY   What about all the drunken ghosts in here? They chose, all the Dick Firhams. They signed up, they couldn't wait to get shot.

JIM   They didn't know what they were doing.

SALLY   Do you?

JIM   They were young. They had no imagination. They couldn't imagine hell.

SALLY   Can you?

JIM   No I can't. I know all about hell, I've read the brochure, I just can't imagine it.

SALLY   Come on, you've had a wank over Gloria Hunniford.

JIM   Lack of imagination. That's what'll do for us.

SALLY   Either that or too much.

JIM   There's an amazing bit in this book. I'll read it to you.

(*The bugle sound of the Last Post is heard, offstage.*)

JIM   On July 17th, Lieutenant J. Annan of the First Battalion . . .

SALLY   The Last Post at the Menin Gate. Don't you want to nip up and see it?

JIM   Do you mind?

(SALLY *gestures as if to say 'Go'.* JIM *exits, and the Last Post begins to change, a jazzy trumpet variation on it. This is taken over by a slow thundering of big guns building and erupting suddenly into very loud explosions. Spectacular lights from the shelling, and the explosions continue even louder.* SALLY *stands alone in the middle of it, aghast and confused. It seems like she might be killed. A man appears and sweeps her to the ground, shouting "Get down, for God's sake". The explosions subside and the lighting returns to normal. He runs her from the centre to the edge of the stage. They are both out of breath. He pushes her back and aims his gun at her.*)

JASPER   What are you?

(SALLY *can't speak.*)

What are you? Are you German? Deutch? Are you a woman?

SALLY   Fuck mine.

JASPER   You speak English?

SALLY   Fucking hell. What was all that? Who are you?

JASPER   Perhaps you haven't noticed. I am pointing a
            gun at your head. I think I am in a better
            position than you to ask questions.

SALLY   It's not a real gun is it?

            (*She laughs. He is taken aback by this, laughs,
            then sits down, laughing slightly hysterically as
            the lights fade. Distant guns are heard.*)

                        Scene Eight

JASPER *is eyeing* SALLY *warily, still pointing the gun at her,
but now less so.*

SALLY   Jim? Jim? Jim can you come out now!

JASPER   Jim?

SALLY   Yes!

JASPER   Jim Kirk the quartermaster?

SALLY   It's a film. Is it a movie? Where are the cameras?
            It's TV. Are you the presenter?

JASPER   What language are you speaking? Are you
            Flemish?

            (SALLY *wipes her nose with her hand and mainly
            sobs but partly laughs.*)

SALLY   Yes. No. I'm English.

            (*She moves to pick up her handbag.* JASPER
            prevents this, and kicks the bag away. SALLY
            sobs.)

SALLY   Please stop this. Please.

JASPER   (*softening*) You are a woman. I don't intend to
            hurt you.

SALLY   You won't will you?

            (*He puts his gun down.*)

JASPER   What are these clothes? Are you injured?

SALLY   No.

JASPER   Are you in a funk? You are a woman. You must
            be funky.

            (SALLY *mostly laughs, but still sobbing.*)

            What are you doing here?

SALLY   I'm on holiday.

            (*Now it's* JASPER'S *turn to laugh.*)

JASPER   Maybe I'm funky.

SALLY   I'm sure you are.

            (JASPER *looks around.*)

JASPER   I don't appear to be in the same place as I was.

SALLY   Nor do I.

JASPER   It's so green.

SALLY   There are no buildings.

            (JASPER *sits down.*)

JASPER   You and I need to have a conversation.

SALLY   Yes.

JASPER   Do you agree that we are in Belgium?

SALLY   Yes.

JASPER   And we are in the reserve line?

SALLY   No. I told you, I'm on holiday.

JASPER   You came on holiday to the Western Front?

SALLY   Western Front. When do you think this is?

JASPER   Monday.

SALLY   Yes.

JASPER   June.

SALLY   Yes.

JASPER   The fourteenth.

SALLY   Yes.

SALLY   }   1988.

JASPER   1916.

     (*Blackout. Music.*)

Scene Nine

Some sort of limbo. Lights up again. JASPER *is still pointing the gun at her but in a less aggressive way.*

SALLY   I live in London now.

JASPER   Which part of London?

SALLY   Streatham, well more Brixton really.

JASPER   Brixton is not in London. Which road do you live in Brixton?

SALLY   New Park Road.

JASPER   I know Brixton. There is not a road called New Park Road in Brixton.

SALLY   Yes there is.

JASPER   I'm sure there isn't.

SALLY   Well tell that to my postman, he keeps delivering letters there. Listen, New Park Road probably had a different name when you were there.

     (*Pause.*)

JASPER   If you are from 1988 you know perhaps about this war?

SALLY   Not much. You should ask my old man. He's
             obsessed by it. I'm not really bothered myself.
             Don't worry, you win in the end. Well, we win I
             suppose.

JASPER   When does it end?

SALLY   1918. November, I think.

             (*Long pause. He relaxes more.*)

JASPER   Do chaps still play cricket in 1988?

SALLY   Oh yeah cricket. Chaps still play. I quite like
             cricket, good for sunbathing.

JASPER   Sunbathing.

SALLY   I suppose you've got wotsisname . . . that old
             cricketer with the big beard, W. C. Fields . . .

JASPER   (*amused*) W. G. Grace.

SALLY   W. G. Grace, that's it.

JASPER   W. G. I saw him play once, just before he
             retired.

SALLY   Really?

JASPER   No, my father was going to take me but I felt
             under the weather.

SALLY   Under the weather.

JASPER   That seems very long ago.

SALLY   It was longer ago for me.

JASPER   W. G. at Lords. (*He works it out.*) Eleven B. T.

SALLY   British Telecom.

JASPER   Before trenches. A joke we have. What is
             British Telecom?

SALLY   It's a joke we have. Telephones, you have them,
             don't you?

JASPER   Yes, some people.

SALLY   We all have one in 1988. No one writes letters
              any more.

JASPER   So who is this postman in New Park Road?

SALLY   He comes by once a day with a big pile of
              letters from banks and mail order companies and
              don't ask me to explain mail order, take it from
              me it's nothing to do with getting men through
              the post, more's the pity.

JASPER   Once a day?

SALLY   Twice.

JASPER   At home there are four posts a day.

SALLY   Well bully for you.

JASPER   Yes bully for me. Bully beef, bully beef.

SALLY   Sunday wouldn't be Sunday without a bit of
              bully.

              (*Pause.*)

              This is weird.

JASPER   What age are you?

SALLY   Twenty nine. And you?

JASPER   Nineteen.

SALLY   You look older.

              (*Pause.*)

JASPER   So, I am not only ten years younger, I'm also
              sixty two years older than you.

SALLY   Yes.

JASPER   This is queer.

SALLY   Queer, yes. What are we going to find on the
              other side of those hills? When is it going to be,

1916, 1988? Maybe it's in the middle. God I hope not.

JASPER   In the middle is 1952.

SALLY   Pendant!

JASPER   Pendant. Ah, I see.

SALLY   (*reminded*) I don't like this. I'm scared. I'm frightened.

JASPER   I'm not. I'm quite content. Wherever I am must be better than where I was. One instant I was being shelled, possibly about to die, the next I find myself in some sort of peace-time place with a strange and beautiful woman.

SALLY   Where's this beautiful woman then?

          (*They both laugh.*)

          We should go and find where we are.

JASPER   Yes, I'm tired.

          (*He relaxes. He is suddenly very tired.*)

SALLY   Do you want a cigarette?

JASPER   Yes, thank you. (*She gives him one, and he stares at it.*) What's this? It looks like this cigarette is wearing a skirt.

SALLY   That's the filter.

JASPER   What does it do?

SALLY   Well, I don't know, it filters out some of the bad stuff. You probably don't realise this but cigarettes give you cancer.

JASPER   Cancer. Like a cancer?

SALLY   I suppose so. Anyway cigarettes kill you.

JASPER   Cigarettes kill you? Let them.

(*He smokes a little. Then goes to sleep.* SALLY *takes the cigarette out of his hand and stubs it out. She 'arranges' him more comfortably. Music plays as the lights fade, a dreamy variation on the previous piece.*)

Scene Ten

SALLY   But you actually joined up?

JASPER   Yes, I joined up. I enlisted. Who is W. C . Fields?

SALLY   Joined up. You joined up. Like your hands and your feet have been sewn together. Joined up. I wouldn't have joined up.

JASPER   Women can't.

SALLY   Yes we can. But even if I was a man I wouldn't.

JASPER   You'd have to. There's conscription now.

SALLY   I still wouldn't.

JASPER   Then you'd be put in prison.

SALLY   I don't care.

JASPER   Then you'd be shot.

SALLY   Really?

JASPER   I have a friend, Jack, who is in, curiously, Brixton Prison and . . .

SALLY   That's just near New Park Road.

JASPER   He's a conchie. He expects to be shot any day now.

SALLY   But you chose to go.

JASPER   Yes. It was my duty.

SALLY   (*contemptuous*) Duty.

JASPER	If one has in general benefited from the laws of one's country, one is not morally entitled to reject those laws if they suddenly do not suit.
SALLY	Fancy phrase. Bit pat. Did you learn it at school?
JASPER	Are there no wars in your time?
SALLY	Not much at the moment. Iran-Iraq.
JASPER	(*as one word*) IranIraq. I've never heard of that. (*Belches.*) IranIraq.
SALLY	(*a bit disgusted*) Argh! Is that some First World War game?
JASPER	First World War. First World War. First World War?
SALLY	(*realising*) That's true, I suppose you couldn't call it the First World War until you'd had the second.
JASPER	And the third?
SALLY	Not yet.
JASPER	We call it the Great War.
SALLY	I know. It makes me laugh. Why not go mad and call it the Absolutely Brilliant War.
JASPER	World, it's not truthfully world is it? Turkey, Africa a little, the Middle East somewhat, does it become bigger?
SALLY	I don't know. I always think of it just being in France and Belgium.
JASPER	So what is the Second World War? When does it happen?
SALLY	It starts in 1939. I suppose you don't know Adolf Hitler (*He doesn't.*) Well he becomes leader of Germany and Germany invades lots of other countries and we end up fighting them.
JASPER	That's the same as this war.

SALLY   Is it?

JASPER   If we win this one how can we let the Germans start another war so soon?

SALLY   I don't know, it's not my fault, is it? Listen we must go.

JASPER   Where?

              (*Music plays as the lights fade on* SALLY *and* JASPER.)

Scene Eleven

Back at the cafe. JIM *enters, reading from a book.*

JIM   In July 1917, Lieutenant J. Annan of the First Battalion Royal Scots describes the scene at Minty Farm. "Minty Farm was a strong point, an outpost fortified by Germans and bristling with machine guns, but the Gordons had taken it. They took it with the bayonet, like wild things and when we got to it, the dead were lying all around. Germans grey against the mud, all mixed up with the dead Gordons lying there in their kilts."

Lieutenant J. Annan. In the heat of battle when he must have been more scared, more excited if you like, than any of us here has ever been, he didn't just think: "Oh Jesus, look at all these bodies," he thought, "Oh Jesus, look at all these bodies, and look how some are grey and some are bright tartan, and the grey matches the mud." Of course, for him the First World War didn't take place in black and white.

Two sentences later. (*Reads.*) "As we were struggling up to the farm, one of the boys got hit with a huge shell fragment. It sliced him in two. He dropped his rifle and bayonet and threw his arms up in the air, and the top part of his torso fell back onto the ground. The unbelievable thing was that the legs and the kilt went on running, just like a chicken with its head chopped off! One of my boys - I think it was his special pal - went rushing after him. He had some mad idea of picking up the upper part of the torso and chasing the legs to join him up. I shouted him back and he was wild with me because he wanted to help his pal. He couldn't realise he was beyond help."

Absurd. Tragic. And funny, isn't it? Really, just a pair of legs in a kilt sprinting through the mud of Belgium, and his 'special pal', surely some euphemism for his gay lover, rushing behind the legs gripping the torso. It's like some psychopathic Benny Hill sketch. But it isn't because they weren't playing for laughs, it REALLY HAPPENED on July 31st 1917 at seven thirty five in the morning. Where is that woman? Where is that bloody woman?

(*The lights change.*)

Scene Twelve

SALLY *and* JASPER *are walking.*

JASPER Margaret Thatcher? A woman.

SALLY Yes. You're right to be appalled, but you're appalled for the wrong reason. Jasper, let's stop for a while, I'm knackered. We've walked miles.

JASPER About two I would estimate.

SALLY We don't seem to be getting anywhere.

JASPER How can a woman be a Prime Minister of England? Women are not permitted to vote, surely never to stand for Parliament.

SALLY They are in 1988, matey boy. I can't really see your problem. What about Queen Victoria? Or Elizabeth the First?

JASPER   The First?

SALLY   There's another Elizabeth coming up.

JASPER   A woman can be the head of state but no woman has the necessary brain to be a politician.

SALLY   Yes we have. We can vote, we can swear, we can be the fucking Prime Minister if we want. We can be doctors and road sweepers, we can be lesbians and have abortions, we can make passes at men, we can bring up children on our own, we can fart and sweat, we can do what we want. Or we could if it weren't for people like you, men who still think like you.

JASPER   There can be no future for a world where women have such rights.

SALLY   Oh come off it, you pompous git. I'll grant you, you have got a very reasonable excuse for having old-fashioned views, but think about it, think of the women you know, your mother, your sweetheart, your sister, are they not, at heart, as good as you?

JASPER   My mother, my sweetheart, my sister. I have none of those. I had a sweetheart.

SALLY   What happened?

JASPER   She met another chap. (*He shrugs.*)

SALLY   You're probably a virgin aren't you?

     (*He blushes.*)

SALLY   Oh how sad, you may die never having had your leg over.

JASPER   Leg over?

SALLY   (*rummaging in her handbag*) I'm hungry. What about you?

JASPER   Of course I'm hungry.

(*She finds a Kit Kat. Breaks it. Gives him half. He looks at it suspiciously.*)

SALLY   Kit Kat, don't worry, just eat it.

(*He does.*)

JASPER   Sally, I am in love with you.

SALLY   I never realised Kit Kats were so potent.

JASPER   I'm in love with you.

SALLY   Don't be stupid. It's very flattering. You're nineteen and I'm the first women you've seen for three months and the woman you fancied refused to fuck you.

JASPER   (*amazed*) The way that you talk. You swear . . .

SALLY   Like a trooper? Are you afraid of me?

JASPER   In the past three months every moment of every day. I could have been killed . . . (*Clicks fingers.*) . . . like that. I'm not afraid of a woman, even one who comes from the future. This time tomorrow I may be dead. Of course I am afraid of you.

SALLY   What you mean by "I love you" is, that in your world you have to say that before you can do the business. I mean pre-marital sex is not on in 1914, is it?

JASPER   1916. There are brothels for us, my pals visit them. I could, I have been tempted but . . . (*Shrugs.*) I want . . . I want . . . I want you.

SALLY   I already have a boyfriend.

JASPER   Yes, but he won't object, he hasn't been born yet.

SALLY   It's unimaginable.

JASPER   You wouldn't want me to die a virgin.

SALLY   You may not die. I've heard lots of old blokes talking about the First World War, *they* survived it.

JASPER   It's unlikely you would have heard from the ones who didn't. Look at you: to me you are the most exotic creature imaginable. The clothes you are wearing, the cuss words you use, you're shocking. I have been shocked but you bring an entirely new understanding . . .

SALLY   It's fairly shocking for me too you know. It's not everyday you're thrown - oh look . . .

JASPER   Good God! What is that?

SALLY   It is the most beautiful thing.

JASPER   It's some new weapon the Huns have got.

SALLY   No, no, I know what it is, it's beautiful, I'm home, it's a pylon.

(*Music.* SALLY *and* JASPER *exit. Lights fade.*)

Scene Thirteen

The music fades and the lights rise on SALLY *sitting in a pub.* JIM *arrives with two pints of beer.*

SALLY   I don't want another one.

JIM   You haven't got one. I've got two. All that humping's given me a thirst.

SALLY   Yes, I didn't realise I had so much stuff left at your place.

JIM   Jesus I'm hot.

SALLY   So how have you been?

JIM   Shit.

SALLY   How's the firm?

JIM   Shit.

SALLY   How's the shit?

JIM   Firm. (*He laughs, despite himself.*) I've missed
            you.

SALLY   You probably won't believe this but I've missed
            you too.

JIM   When?

SALLY   Sometimes.

JIM   The only time I don't miss you is when I'm
            asleep. Because if I'm not too pissed to dream,
            you turn up sometimes all mixed up with Belgian
            policemen and passports and pastis. Then I wake
            up and you and everyone rush off the stage.
            And then there's a tiny moment, an instant when
            I seem to be conscious for the first time in my
            life and I don't know what sex I am, I don't even
            know what species I am. An infinitesimally small
            vacuum where everything is possible. And then
            it crashes in, you're not there. I miss you, it's
            Thursday and I've got hours to go before I'll
            sleep again and all those hours will be spent
            missing you.

            (SALLY, *moved by his speech, touches him.*)

JIM   The only other time I don't miss you is when
            I'm aiming darts at your photo.

SALLY   Would you rather I went? Jim! No, no. I'm sorry.
            Let's play fisties for something.

JIM   I just haven't talked about it to anyone much.
            There's only so much maudlin self-pity my
            friends can take. Then they put their hands in
            their pockets and pull out the old cliches, "it'll
            wear off", "time is the great healer", here's a
            good one, "he who loves most is the inferior and
            must suffer".

SALLY   "Better to have loved and lost than never to
            have loved at all."

JIM   Yeah. Good. "Men have died and worms have eaten them, but not for love."

SALLY   "There's plenty more fish in the sea".

JIM   The timeless classic. Plenty more fish - I suppose they're all true.

SALLY   Most people have felt like you at one time or another.

JIM   That one really pisses me off. I want my suffering to be unique. I want it to be cliche-resistant, but it's just another bog-ordinary broken heart. Another doomed love affair. Join the queue, here's a handful of homespun philosophy. Now fuck off. They're bored by it. I was talking to Gary, after five minutes his eyes glazed over and he started talking about his car and the end of the Iran-Iraq War . . .

SALLY   Has it ended?

JIM   Gary says I'm wallowing in it and he's right. I'm aware of all the dangers. The heavy drinking, losing interest in everything, not taking care of yourself. It's hard, but I am deliberately doing all those things. I've got drunk religiously every night since you left, and some mornings. I've worn the same pair of socks for a week. It's not easy becoming a derelict but I'm trying. I'm trying to become as pathetic as possible for you, Sally, for you.

SALLY   You have changed. I don't think I've ever seen you so passionate.

JIM   Not even about the First World War?

(SALLY *reacts, on the defensive.*)

JIM   What happened in Belgium? What happened?

SALLY   I don't know. I'm not sure. Something extraordinary, something amazing.

JIM   What?

SALLY   I can't say. I can't tell you about it.

JIM   Well mime it then. One moment we were
            together and the next . . . (*Clicks his fingers.*)
            What happened?

SALLY   You won't believe me.

JIM   Try me.

SALLY   It's too ridiculous.

JIM   Tell me anyway.

SALLY   Promise me you won't laugh and you won't ask
            me any questions?

JIM   Tell me.

SALLY   Promise.

JIM   I promise.

SALLY   I'm going out with your grandad.

            (*Pause.*)

JIM   I haven't laughed.

            (*Music, and the lights fade.*)

Scene Fourteen

SALLY'S *flat.*

JASPER *is wearing* SALLY'S *clothes which make him look
faintly ridiculous and sweet. There are some books open. He
is looking out of a window when something surprises him. He
breaks away from the window.*

JASPER *wanders around, eventually lying centre stage.*

JASPER   Ten!

(*He starts doing press-ups and counting.* SALLY
*enters. She takes her coat off and slides in
under him. He stops the press-ups.*)

SALLY   No, don't stop Jasper.

JASPER   Four!

(*Blackout. The sound of "Whiz-Bang" firing,
exploding. Lights come back on. They're half-
dressed,* SALLY *lying on top of him.*)

SALLY   I must say you've got a lot of energy for a man
          who was born in the nineteenth century. How
          were you on your own? You didn't go out, did
          you?

JASPER   No, I considered it, but there was too much to
          distract me here. Most things look familiar but
          they are made from different materials. There's a
          great deal of . . . of what your 'disposal' razors
          are made of.

SALLY   Plastic.

JASPER   Plastic.

SALLY   (*feeling his cheek*) Did you shave? I can't tell.

JASPER   No I didn't.

SALLY   Why not?

JASPER   I thought I shouldn't. It said on the plastic
          container the plastic razors were in, 'Ladyshave'.

SALLY   Stupid. So you spent all day not shaving?

JASPER   I looked out of the window. So many motorcars
          and all the people, they all seemed to be
          blackies.

SALLY   Don't say blackies, Jasper.

JASPER   So do you shave?

SALLY	We don't say blackies. They're black people. They're the same as you and me.
JASPER	No they aren't, they're black.
SALLY	Yes, but I mean they're human beings.
JASPER	I never suggested otherwise. They're the ones who are brave enough to walk down the road, not me. Black people, blackies - what's the difference - I was just surprised to see so many niggers.
SALLY	I'm going to have to re-educate you baby.
JASPER	What do you mean?
SALLY	Well for example you've obviously never seen a black person.
JASPER	I didn't say that. I saw many coloured men in Flanders, my friend Jack had a coloured doctor, the Mayor of Battersea is a negro.
SALLY	Really?
JASPER	Now, in 1988, I may appear naive, but I am not stupid.
SALLY	No you're not stupid. (*Notices books. Picks up encyclopedia.*) Have you been reading my encyclopedia?
JASPER	Yes, I looked myself up.
SALLY	Did you get a mention?
JASPER	No. There were no Everlys at all. I would have been between the 'Everglades National Park' and 'Chris Evert', a women who appears to merit an entry because she's good at tennis.

(SALLY *looks at the encyclopedia.*)

SALLY	Yes, it's quite new this. Jim gave it to me.
JASPER	(*taking it from her*) I think it must be American.

SALLY   Yes, everything else is. What did you do after that?

JASPER   I managed to ignite the . . . (*Points.*) . . .

SALLY   Television.

JASPER   Television. Extraordinary. How often does it happen?

SALLY   What do you mean? Whenever you turn it on, it happens.

JASPER   It happens every day.

SALLY   And every night. There's always something on.

JASPER   But what purpose does it serve?

SALLY   I don't know, to entertain you, inform you.

JASPER   How did you get one?

SALLY   Everyone's got one.

JASPER   (*incredulous*) Everyone?!

SALLY   Was the Mayor of Battersea really black?

JASPER   Look it up. Did you bring any cigarettes?

SALLY   Yes, here you are. And I bought you a present.

JASPER   Oh a present. How topping.

(*She gives him a bag. There is a shirt in it.*)

SALLY   I hope you like it. I got it cheap in the market.

(*He takes his top off, and puts the shirt on. It's too big.*)

SALLY   Oh dear, it's too big.

JASPER   It's enormous.

SALLY   (*adjusting the sleeves*) Look at the sleeves. Look at the sleeves.

JASPER   (*remembering*) Yes I look like . . . (*Stops
                himself.*) . . . Maxie London? "Got any apples?"
                (*Which was Maxie's catchphrase.* SALLY *shakes
                her head.*)

JASPER   No, he wasn't in the encyclopedia either. Nor
                anyone else I know. I thought Jack might have
                been.

SALLY   Jack? With the coloured doctor?

                (JASPER *nods.*)

                Was he a friend of yours?

                (JASPER *tries to think what he might say about
                Jack. He can't say anything.*)

SALLY   Listen, take the top off and I'll alter the sleeves
                for you.

JASPER   I'll take my shirt off if you take yours off.

SALLY   I'm not wearing a shirt.

JASPER   Not for long, no.

                (*He advances. They kiss. Blackout. "Wizz-bang"
                firing and explosion. Lights up.*)

JASPER   There are some things to be said for 1988.

SALLY   And for 1916. You're very safe sex indeed.

JASPER   Safe sex?

SALLY   Listen Jasper. I don't know how long you are
                going to be with me. And I know you are a long
                way from home. I'm going to have to be your
                teacher and your mum. The only time you can
                be equal to me is at the point of mutual orgasm.
                At all other times you are innocent and hopeless.
                And that, I'm sorry to say, may be why I love
                you. That and your very young, very supple
                body.

                (*He approaches her again.*)

No Jasper no, not again. (*Sings*.) Oh sir Jasper do not touch me, oh Sir Jasper do . . .

(*Music, and the lights fade.*)

Scene Fifteen

JIM   Oh there have been some great wars along the way, but I think the best war there has ever been was the Trojan War. It was such a great war that it was plural. The Trojan Wars. Even the Second World War never got an 's' on the end. The Trojan Wars were so great because of why they started - Paris ran away with Helen - that is to say, they started the wars because someone nicked someone else's girlfriend. It doesn't seem enough of a reason does it? Maybe it does. What would we do if Gadafi abducted Lady Di?

One tactic is certain: the British Army will never stick a load of SAS men inside an immense wooden horse and then try and smuggle it into Tripoli. They wouldn't, would they? A wooden horse? Leave it out Homer, no one buys that shit.

Oh yes but it really happened, or something like it happened, but now it's in colour with Kirk Douglas and Charlton Heston. The first of the 'wars to end all wars', but it's so far away it's a kids story, a pantomime with Agamemnon and Menalaeus as the ugly sisters, and Dobbin the pantomime wooden horse.

I can picture the meal I had five hours ago, if you're interested . . . fishfingers, chips, and beans, but it doesn't seem to have had much effect, because I'm hungry again now. When I finished the meal I didn't feel hungry. At the time the fishfingers, chips and beans seemed like the meal to end all meals. I knew I would have to eat again but I couldn't feel it.

You see footage of the First World War on TV
from time to time, less often than before because
there are new wars to watch now, wars in colour.
But when you see them all you notice how poor
the quality of the film is, or how quaint the
clothes are. Shadows flicker past and we can't
realise they were once human beings.
They will, you can't believe it but I bet they
will, in the end they'll make a sit-com about
Auschwitz.

And Paris ran away with Helen.
And Jasper ran away with Sally.

(*Blackout. Music.*)

Scene Sixteen

JASPER *is picking up split furniture.*

JASPER   In 1988 in England, or as it is now called, Britain,
           it would seem that everything is bad for you.
           Smoking is bad for you, alcohol is bad for you,
           milk is bad for you, sexual intercourse is bad for
           you, water is bad for you, meat is bad for you,
           running is bad for you, not running is bad for
           you, eggs are bad for you, cheese is bad for
           you, breathing in the street is bad for you, the
           twentieth century is bad for you.

           It is of no interest to me because I know what *is*
           bad for you - being shot through the head is bad
           for you.

(*Lights change. Music.*)

Scene Seventeen

SALLY'S *flat.* SALLY *and* JASPER.

JASPER   So how many false moustaches do you own?

SALLY   Only two. I've got a handlebar and a Hitler. I've
           told you about Hitler.

JASPER   Oh yes. I should think I know more about Adolf
            Hitler than you. Did you know he's a
            vegetarian? Was a vegetarian. And he took
            cocaine.

SALLY   No.

JASPER   He took pills all the time. He couldn't sleep.
            That's what I read.

SALLY   Must be one of Jim's books.

JASPER   And I've discovered he's in my war too.

SALLY   Who, Jim?

JASPER   Hitler. He is in France throughout 1917. If only
            he had been killed. It would have saved you all
            a great deal of trouble. Although you wouldn't
            have that absolute figure of evil to match
            yourselves so favourably against. Nor would you
            have two false moustaches.

SALLY   So pompous.

JASPER   And so young.

SALLY   I bought you a present.

JASPER   Oh a present. How topping.

            (*She gives him an old photo.*)

SALLY   It's an old photo.

            (JASPER *looks at it, then at her.*)

JASPER   Good Lord, it's Captain Johnson!

SALLY   You know him? Really?

JASPER   No of course not. That's what you wanted
            though, isn't it? I'm a soldier from The Great
            War, he's a soldier from the Great War, we must
            know each other. Such a small lost world. We all
            went to each others' houses for tea.

SALLY   I didn't mean it like that. You know we're from
          the same country. Your war hasn't been
          forgotten. (*She kisses him.*) Can you put your
          shirt on? He'll be here in a minute.

JASPER   Why? From what I understand of 1988, it's really
          quite good form to cavort naked in the home.

SALLY   I don't know, Jim might . . . oh fuck it, doesn't
          matter. Why are you so spiky tonight anyway?

JASPER   You know how difficult it is for me to meet your
          people. It's fraught with danger. And this is your
          'old man'. The man I snatched you away from.
          The man whose passport I stole. The man you
          left stranded in Belgium. The man who would
          probably like to kill me.

SALLY   He couldn't kill a fly.

JASPER   That's what I thought once.

SALLY   You'll probably like him. You're both hopeless
          and he's fascinated by your bloody war.

SALLY   What have you told him about me?

SALLY   I told him something stupid.

JASPER   What?

SALLY   I said you were his grandad.

JASPER   I beg your pardon?

SALLY   I didn't want to say something that was a
          complete lie.

JASPER   It is a complete lie.

SALLY   It might not be. Maybe you go back and have
          a family and he's your grandson.

JASPER   Maybe I'm your grandad. Perhaps I'm
          everybody's bloody grandad.

SALLY   Well it's easier than being everybody's bloody mother.

                (*The doorbell is heard, off.*)

                Look, it was just a stupid thing I said, he's bound to have forgotten it. He won't be here long. He's just coming round to borrow a moustache and then he's off to a party.

                (SALLY *exits to answer the door.* JASPER *picks up his shirt and puts it on. She re-enters with* JIM. *He is wearing a scruffy First World War uniform and carrying a plastic bag. He puts the bag down.* JASPER *stands up, a bit shocked.* SALLY *is also confused and worried about* JASPER'S *reaction.*)

SALLY   Jasper, Jim.

                (JIM *salutes.*)

JIM   At ease. So, grandad how are you? You're looking good for a man who's been dead for seventy three years.

SALLY   You're pissed aren't you?

                (JIM *removes a can of beer from the plastic bag and opens it.*)

JIM   No I'm not. I've had six pints. Or eight. I'm pissed. I don't want this. (*He puts it down.*)

SALLY   I'll get you a pint of water and a coffee.

                (*She exits.*)

JIM   Yes I do. (*Picks beer up. He and* JASPER *eye each other.*) Do you know she told me once to go to a disco and call the bouncer a cunt? Do you know that? What do you think of that? Actually I like bouncers, they're always so sober and helpful. They're not violent. They deflect you home. Jasper, Jasper, I don't hate you, Jasper. I love you in fact. I love you. I love

everybody when I'm pissed. Have you ever
taken amyl nitrate Jasper? Life's a hoot when
you're pissed, Jasper. Do you know in the First
World War they used to get them pissed before
they went over the top? It doesn't hurt so much
when you're pissed, Jasper, "See if you can get
it there between my eyes".

A couple of weeks ago I fell off a balcony,
about twenty feet. And I didn't break a bone in
my body. Do you know why? Because my body
was supple. And it was supple because I was
pissed. The fact is, of course, that if I hadn't
been pissed, I wouldn't have fallen off the
balcony in the first place. You're not saying
much Jasper, in fact you're saying nothing. I
have no idea what your voice is like even. I
should think it's high and a bit upper class, is it?

JASPER   Are you what I become?

JIM   It is! I was right! Bravo! Am I what you become?
         Are you what I was?

         (SALLY *re-enters.*)

         Ah thank God for the timely interruption! If only
         life could be like that. "About your overdraft Mr
         Simpson it's . . . " (*Accent.*) "I'm sorry, Police,
         we're going to have to clear the bank, there's
         been a bomb scare".

SALLY   What are you talking about?

JIM   I'm talking about everything that comes into my
         head. I'm on auto-talk.

SALLY   Why do I always go out with men who talk all
         the time?

JIM   Bollocks. Jasper's hardly said a word. And
         Jasper's my grandad. And your grandad's
         supposed to be a repository of wisdom. Come on
         Jasper, tell me how I should lead my life, that's
         what grandads do isn't it? Come on, some
         Edwardian homily so I can cope more easily with

the world. What is it you know that I don't? Why
did she leave me for you? Come on Jasper.
Grandad. We've got something in common.
We've shared the twentieth century and we've
both had our cocks inside her.

SALLY   Why don't you take the false moustache and go?

JIM   I'm sorry (*Sits down*). Do you know I was
             looking through my address book the other day.
             Three of the people in it are dead. Vernon, a
             bloke I knew in college, he died of meningitis.
             Janice, a women I made love to once, died in a
             car crash. My grandmother, she died of being
             very old. Technically it's two and a half, my
             grandad can still be contacted on the same
             number. My other grandad, the one who's dead,
             is standing here. How many people in your
             address book are dead? Eh, Jasper? It's not a
             bad average. I know maybe three hundred
             people and three of them are dead. I know two
             hundred and ninety seven people, therefore.
             And then there's John Keats, Wolfgang Mozart,
             Alexander The Great, Jesus Christ, Minnie
             Ripperton. Do you know what they all have in
             common?

SALLY   No, Jim, we don't.

JIM   They all died younger than I am now. On my
             thirty seventh birthday I compiled a list of all the
             people who died before the age of thirty seven.
             At first I went through the encyclopedia. Then I
             thought, yes, they've all died young but they've
             got their way into the encyclopedia, the bastards.
             I'm not going to, am I? I doubt I'll even get an
             obituary, I might manage a paragraph in the
             Hackney Gazette: "Jim Simpson, who lived
             locally, has died." The end. Wrong to look in
             the encyclopedia for people to outlive. Soldiers
             in the war, they're the ones - they've done sod-
             all other than die pointlessly. Thomas Bowlby,
             died aged twenty four, idiot! Maurice Atkinson,
             twenty one, you fucking wanker Maurice, I've
             already beaten you by sixteen years!

I reckon if I die tonight, which, let's be honest, must be on the cards, I'll get a much bigger turnout at my funeral than if I die when I'm eighty when I'm old, forgotten and my friends have all died. Will you go to my funeral? Sally?

SALLY   Please leave Jim, please.

JIM   Sally, I'm HIV positive.

           (*Pause.*)

SALLY   No you're not.

JIM   I might be.

SALLY   You're pathetic.

JASPER   What do you know? You know nothing.

JIM   Here's what I fucking know.

           (*He pulls out a gun and points it at his own head. SALLY screams. Then he points it at JASPER who deftly, and a bit brutally, disarms him.*)

           No, it's not real. I got it with the uniform. It's a theatrical gun.

           (*Blackout. Music.*)

Scene Eighteen

A party. Loud music plays, Plastique Bertrand.

JASPER   (*talking to invisible woman*) Yes, yes, I agree. Plastic Bertrand. Jasper. Yes it is rather isn't it? And yourself? Good evening Miranda. Oh I'm, I don't really do a great deal at present. I'm unemployed. Really? Yes I came with Sally, Sally Hunt, do you know her? Ah, look, here she comes. Very pleasant. Goodbye.

SALLY   Are you ok?

JASPER   Yes, yes I'm fine.

SALLY   I'm sorry, I didn't mean to ignore you. I had to talk to Jenny.

JASPER   What is PR? Miranda said she was "in PR." Is that bad?

SALLY   (*laughs to herself*) Yes it is, pretty bad.

JASPER   I'd like to go.

SALLY   Are you ok? Did she upset you?

JASPER   No. She was a little disconcerting.

SALLY   Disconcerting.

JASPER   It's hard to accustom oneself, I mean I don't know her and so much of her body on display.

SALLY   Yes, from a flash of ankle to a lingering close up of thighs. It must be hard.

JASPER   Yes it is.

SALLY   Seems a shame to waste it. Shall we go home?

JASPER   I am very tired.

SALLY   Well let's go then. (*She begins to exit.*) Come on. Do you want to go or not? What's the matter? You've been very quiet this evening. What's the matter?

JASPER   (*he sits down*) I telephoned the Imperial War Museum this afternoon, I asked about Jasper Everly.

SALLY   (*to another guest*) Bye Jen, I'll phone you later. What did they say?

JASPER   At present I don't know. They said they'd find out. I have to go there on Monday.

SALLY   Is that a good idea? Do you want to know what happens to you?

JASPER   Of course . . . I don't know.

SALLY   I don't know if I'd want to. I went to a fortune-teller once.

JASPER   What did she say?

SALLY   It doesn't matter what she said. The thing is I could choose to disregard it if I wanted. She didn't really know did she? I mean you . . .

JASPER   Yes it's already happened. Someone will be able to look you up eventually. "There's a divinity shapes our ends . . . "

SALLY   " . . . Rough hew them how we may". Jim used to say that. There's a divinity . . . Jim, I wonder how he is?

JASPER   Perhaps he is, what do you say? HIV positive. Perhaps you are too therefore. And me. Perhaps I die of AIDS sixty years before anyone else. Perhaps I start the disease.

SALLY   Don't be so flippant.

JASPER   AIDS. (*Shrugs.*) I read that twenty thousand people died of syphilis in 1920.

SALLY   Twenty thousand, that's a lot. Jim isn't HIV positive. Well if he is he doesn't know, he's far too chicken to have found out.

JASPER   Chicken?

SALLY   Scared. Funky. Funky chicken. (*She giggles, shaking her head laughing.*)

JASPER   Don't Sally, Don't. I hate your private jokes. They make me . . . sometimes you really get my goat.

SALLY   It's not easy for me either Jasper. I don't know what I'm doing. (*Pause.*) What do you think they'll say to you on Monday?

JASPER   I can't imagine.

SALLY   What would you like them to say?

JASPER   Jasper Everly, having won the VC, returned
              home after the war, married Enoch Bennett's
              sister Emily, and had three lovely children.
              Medical science was astounded to discover that
              Jasper was not susceptible to illness or ageing.
              Indeed he was declared to be immortal. Two
              years after Emily died peacefully in her sleep,
              he met and married, a girl sixty years younger
              than himself called Sally Hunt with whom he
              lives happily to this day.

              (*He kisses her.*)

SALLY   Who is Emily Bennett?

              (*She kisses him.* JASPER *turns away.*)

SALLY   (*sings*) I don't want to be a soldier,
              I don't want to go to war;
              I'd rather hang around Picadilly Underground,
              Living off the earnings of a painted lady;
              Don't want a bayonet up my arsehole,
              Don't want my bollocks shot away;
              I'd rather stay in England,
              Merry, Merry England,
              and fornicate my fucking life away.

              (*Lights change. Music.*)

Scene Nineteen

Spotlight on JASPER, *in darkness.*

JASPER   Punk, pylons, penicillin, feminism, polyester,
              kebab, shish and doner, Althea and Donna,
              traffic lights, MS, ME, VD, DHSS, LSD, DA,
              BBC, ITV, USSR, friendly fire, Madonna,
              bouncers, the weather forecast, Vietnam, blue
              savers, have a nice day, "have a nice day",
              lager, concentration camps, ring-pull cans,
              condoms, one day game, homogenized, reggae,
              Jeremy Beadle, the News, stand-up comic, the
              Welfare State, the World Cup, Gaye Bikers on

Acid, Jo Orton, ozone, tomato ketchup, the
Common Market, anti-plaque formula, salmonella,
Gary Lineker, panatella, bistro, avocado, yogurt,
Exocet, Chernobyl, Coronation Street,
Paschendale, mangos, nectarines, fishfingers,
television, pylons. "Have a nice day". Sally.

(*Blackout. Music.*)

Scene Twenty

Three spotlights.

SALLY   (*reads*) Dear Jenny. How about this, a letter! I
             haven't written to you since we were in college
             and too skint to phone. I've worked out I've
             only written one proper letter since then, a
             "Dear John" to Skinny Derek. Did I ever tell
             you about old Skinny? I met him in France on a
             beach, he was very thin. He was dying of cancer
             of the throat. We sat by a fire and he had a
             guitar and I know it's corny but he sang to me.
             And his songs were so sad. And I went back to
             where he was staying because I couldn't bear
             for him to be alone with all that unhappiness.
             And then in the morning, when I was leaving, he
             said to me, as honestly as any man has ever
             spoken to me, "You didn't believe all that
             bollocks about cancer did you?"

             I'm sorry about Jasper, Jenny, my toyboy. He
             was a bit off at the party. He's a difficult one.
             You've never understood, have you Jenny, that
             difficult is exciting for me? That's why I fancy
             Jack Nicholson and you fancy Sebastian Coe.
             I'm sorry to get heavy. Happy Breast Feeding!
             All my love, Sally.

             P.S. I know that even you would never really
             fancy Sebastian Coe.

JASPER   (JASPER *is writing*) "Dear Jack."

(*He pauses. Looks up. He doesn't know what to write. He sits back and practices what he might say.*)

Dear Jack . . . Dear Jack, I walked past 103 yesterday. What has your mad father done to your front door? It's yellow! Not only is your front door yellow, it's also orange! Oh you, you must love it.

(*He starts writing again.*)

Dear Jack, I regret not seeing you before I went to Flanders. I was afraid of meeting you, I avoided your house with its black front door. I knew you would belch your disapproval. By the way forget Mesopatania, Jack, Iraq's much easier. (*He tries to belch 'Iraq'.*)

Jack you know I only joined up because I was afraid not to. How could I not? Emily Bennett. Stupid girl. Jack, I cannot tell you what horrors I have seen. I cannot tell you. And I know what happens to you.

I wanted to write to Father, or Geoffrey, but I wrote to you because I knew you wouldn't ignore my letter, just because you were dead.

(*He laughs bitterly and tears up the letter.*)

JIM   (*reads*) Dear Gary, Sorry I didn't make the cricket night but recently I discovered my knob had dropped off, so I am spending some time stitching it back on again. I have been in the wars. I am also taking classes in mediocrity, paying off my overdraft and feeling better about Sally. My life is taking a more even keel. I am back to abject chaos but at least it's my own. Give us a call and we'll get stoned and go to the wrestling again. Yours, Jim.

P.S. . . . I bet a bloke fifty quid today that Margaret Thatcher would still be Prime Minister in 1995. I hope by then I can afford to be wrong.

(*Lights change. Music.*)

Scene Twenty One

SALLY'S *flat.* SALLY *and* JASPER.

JASPER   Missing, believed killed. July, 1916. My name is on the Menin Gate, with all the others. And I have a grave therefore, because even if they don't know who you are, they give you a tombstone, a whole tombstone. For the Germans, it's four to one. "Soldier of the Great War known unto God". A phrase composed by Rudyard Kipling. It translates as, 'there was such a tiny amount of this person's body left that we couldn't tell who it was.' You see no one can identify a person merely by fondling a morsel of their liver. Not even on "You Bet".

SALLY   "You Bet"? What's that?

JASPER   Television. You aren't there for it. When you're not here I watch TV all the time. I have two favourite programmes: "You Bet" and "The News". I died in the Great War.

SALLY   Not if you stay here. 'Missing, believed killed' could be just 'relocated in the future'.

JASPER   Yes.

SALLY   Don't go back to Belgium, Jasper.

JASPER   It's not possible. (*Pause.*) Nothing is possible but everything has happened.

SALLY   You don't want to go back do you?

JASPER   Good God, no. I'd never manage to return without you anyway. I can't do anything without you.

SALLY   I know how foreign it all seems to you.

JASPER   I would have liked to see my father again. I may have had leave before I went missing.

SALLY   Better to stay alive though.

JASPER   Oh yes, yes. Anything to stay alive. I shall have to learn your language. Perhaps eventually I shall be neither innocent nor hopeless. No one will be able to guess my secret - only you. And Jim.

SALLY   Everyone's got a secret.

JASPER   I'll get used to the food. I'll find a job. I can do something, I'm sure. I can "be in PR".

           (SALLY *laughs, somewhat hollow.*)

JASPER   There are thousands, millions of "displaced persons". I'll be just like them.

SALLY   We'll sort it out.

JASPER   There are others like me. I'm just a, what is it, an 'illegal alien', that's all.

SALLY   We'll sort it out. I'm sure we can. We have to.

JASPER   Yes we must. Maybe I'll write to "Jim'll Fix It".

SALLY   I never know what you'll say next.

           (*Lights change. Music.*)

Scene Twenty Two

A pub. JIM *and* JASPER.

JASPER   And then you were always lousy. All of the time. Some of the chaps, the blokes used to spend hours burning the lice off with dog ends, but there were always reinforcements. We used to say 'a louse that's born in the morning is a grandmother by the evening.' We envied those lice though. All that . . .

JIM   How's your father?

JASPER   My father?

JIM   Sex.

JASPER   Sex . . . yes.

JIM   Did you think about sex a lot?

JASPER   No.

JIM   There were brothels for you though weren't there?

JASPER   Yes.

JIM   Did you visit them?

JASPER   Once or twice. Twice.

JIM   War. Isn't it just sex with hate?

JASPER   No.

JIM   Did they really play football in No Man's Land on Christmas Day 1914?

JASPER   Yes I believe so. I'm told the Germans won 4-2. They tried it again the following year but it was prohibited. Chap with the ball got shot by one of his own officers.

JIM   The ultimate red card. People used to get drunk before they went over the top didn't they?

JASPER   So you said.

JIM   Did I?

JASPER   Sometimes there was a tot of rum, I think.

JIM   What was it like, going over?

JASPER   I don't know.

JIM   Did you want to?

JASPER   We had to.

JIM   How did you cope?

JASPER   Pals. Jokes.

JIM   Yes, jokes.

JASPER   After a while you become accustomed to the idea of dying young. Quite soothing.

JIM   I was surprised you wanted to meet me. You know, after the other time. I'm sorry about all that grandad business.

JASPER   (*shrugs*) I couldn't be your grandfather anyway, you're the wrong class. Jim, will you take me to Belgium?

JIM   Why?

JASPER   I have to go back to Belgium. You're the only person who can take me.

JIM   I've got work . . . I mean . . . (*Pointing at JASPER.*) . . . passport?

JASPER   I have one. Not yours. We'll go together. Fix it for me Jim.

(*Blackout. "Jim'll Fix It" music plays.*)

Scene Twenty Three

SALLY *reads from a letter.*

SALLY   Dear Sally, I have gone as you knew I would. I shall miss your world, all the plastic and the luxury. I shall particularly miss the television which was a strange babbling friend to me. It talked but never required an answer. I don't know what I can do in the time that remains but I will try and kill Hitler, I promise. I shall miss you most of course. Thank you Sally for your love and for giving me the most fabulous adventure of my life. Now forget me, slowly. All my love, Jasper Everly. Post script . . . Embarrassing. Apologies if I have given you syphilis.

Scene Twenty Four

Back in Belgium. The sound of a jazzy trumpet segueing into the first part of the Last Post.

JIM *enters, obviously looking at graves.*

JIM   Geoffrey Dearmer died aged twenty one October 29th, 1917 . . . Lieutenant Herbert Richardson, died aged thirty nine June 1915 . . . Soldier of the Great War known unto God . . . Soldier of the Great War known unto God.

SALLY   (*entering*) Maybe that's him.

JIM   (*not knowing she was in Belgium*) Sally!

      (*They hug each other.*)

JIM   He went over. Had to.

      (SALLY *accepts this. Arm in arm together, they look at another grave.*)

JIM   J. McCleod, Royal Scots died aged twenty eight, September 17th, 1916 . . . Jeremy Bennett, Royal Sussex died November 4th, 1917. Bennett. That was my grandmother's maiden name.

SALLY   Bennett? What was her first name?

JIM   Erm. What was it? It began with E . . . Elizabeth. No shorter. Three syllables.

SALLY   Emily. Emily Bennett?

JIM   Emily. That was it, Emily Bennett.

      (*Pause. Music: Last Post.*)

      No Eileen, that's it. Eileen Bennett.

SALLY   Eileen is two syllables.

JIM   Pendant.

(*Spotlight on* JASPER *in uniform.* JASPER *recites MCMXIV by Philip Larkin.*)

JIM   Soldier of the Great War, known unto God.

SALLY   Maybe that's him, the little shit!

(*Blackout.*)